Frederick George Lee

The Other World

Vol. 2

Frederick George Lee

The Other World
Vol. 2

ISBN/EAN: 9783337345914

Printed in Europe, USA, Canada, Australia, Japan

Cover: Foto ©Thomas Meinert / pixelio.de

More available books at **www.hansebooks.com**

The Other World;

OR, GLIMPSES OF THE SUPERNATURAL.

BEING FACTS, RECORDS, AND

TRADITIONS

RELATING TO DREAMS, OMENS, MIRACULOUS OCCURRENCES,
APPARITIONS, WRAITHS, WARNINGS, SECOND-SIGHT,
WITCHCRAFT, NECROMANCY, ETC.

EDITED BY

THE REV. FREDERICK GEORGE LEE, D.C.L.

Vicar of All Saints', Lambeth.

IN TWO VOLUMES. VOL. II.

HENRY S. KING AND CO., LONDON.

1875.

CONTENTS OF VOL. II.

CHAPTER VI.

                                            Page

SPECTRAL Appearances of Persons at the Point of Death and Perturbed Spirits . 1

CHAPTER VII.
Haunted Houses and Localities . . 79

CHAPTER VIII.
Modern Spiritualism 133

CHAPTER IX.
Modern Spiritualism (*continued*) 167

CHAPTER X.
Summary and Conclusion 205

GENERAL INDEX . . . 243

SPECTRAL APPEARANCES.

II.   B

"Now a thing was secretly brought to me, and mine ear received a little thereof.

In thoughts from the visions of the night, when deep sleep falleth on men,

Fear came upon me, and trembling, which made all my bones to shake.

Then a Spirit passed before my face; the hair of my flesh stood up:

It stood still, but I could not discern the form thereof: an Image was before mine eyes."—Job iv. 12-16.

CHAPTER VI.

SPECTRAL APPEARANCES.

EXAMPLES of Spectral Appearances are so numerous, and the Editor has collected so many, both ancient and modern, that considerable difficulty has been occasioned in determining which shall here be set forth. The following, chosen from examples, some well known and well authenticated, and others now first published, but equally interesting and important, and coming to the Editor upon very high authority, deserve the best consideration of the reader.

The following record describes what is known as the "Chester-le-Street" Apparition:—

"About the year of Our Lord 1632 (as near as I can remember, having lost my notes and the copy of the letter to Serjeant Hutton, but I am sure that I do most perfectly remember the substance of the story), near unto Chester-in-the-Street, there lived one Walker, a yeoman of good estate, and a widower, who had a young woman to his kinswoman, that kept his house, who was by the neighbours suspected to be with child, and was, towards the dark of the evening one night, sent away with one Mark Sharp, who was a collier, one who digged coals under ground, and one that had been born at Blackburn hundred in Lancashire; and so she was not heard of a long time, and no noise, or little, was made about it. In the winter time after, one James Graham, or Grime, for so in that country they call them, being a miller, and living about two miles from the place where Walker lived, was one night alone very late in the mill grinding corn; and about twelve or one of the clock at night, he came down the stairs from having been putting corn in the hopper; the mill doors being shut, there stood a woman upon the midst of the floor, with her hair about her head, hanging down and all bloody, with five large wounds on her head. He being much affrighted and amazed began to bless himself;[1] and at last asked her who she was, and what she wanted. To which she said, 'I am the spirit of such a

---

[1] Here in Mr. Surtees' record is a remarkable example of the pious and devout use of the sacred Sign of the Cross, which, having been universal amongst all classes before the Reformation, was continued by many for long generations afterwards, and the use of which since the Catholic Revival in the English Church has become common.

woman who lived with Walker, and being got with child by him, he promised to send me to a private place, where I should be well-looked to, till I was brought to bed, and well again ; and then I should come again and keep his house. And, accordingly,' said the apparition, 'I was one night sent away with one Mark Sharp, who, upon a moor (naming a place that the miller knew) slew me with a pick, such as men dig coals withal and gave me these five wounds, and after threw my body into a coal-pit hard by, and hid the pick under a bank ; and his shoes and stockings being bloody, he endeavoured to wash them ; but seeing the blood would not forth, he hid them there.' And the apparition further told the miller that he must be the man to reveal it, or else that she must still appear and haunt him. The miller returned home very sad and heavy, but spoke not one word of what he had seen, but eschewed as much as he could to stay in the mill within night without company, thinking thereby to escape the seeing again of that frightful apparition. But notwithstanding, one night when it began to be dark, the apparition met him again and seemed very fierce and cruel, and threatened him that if he did not reveal the murder she would continually pursue and haunt him ; yet, for all this, he still concealed it until S. Thomas' Eve before Christmas ; when being soon after sunset walking in his garden, she appeared again, and then so threatened him, and affrighted him, that he promised faithfully to reveal it next morning. In the morning he went to a magistrate, and made the whole matter known with all the circumstances; and diligent search being made, the body was found in a coal-pit, with five wounds in the head, and the pick and shoes and stockings yet bloody; in every circumstance as the apparition had related unto the miller; whereupon Walker and Mark Sharp were both apprehended, but would confess nothing. At the assizes following, I think it was at Durham, they were arraigned, found guilty, condemned and executed; but I could never hear they confessed the fact. There were some that reported the apparition did appear unto the judge, or the foreman of the jury, who was alive in Chester-in-the-Street about ten years ago, as I have been credibly informed, but of that I know no certainty. There are many persons yet alive that can remember this strange murder, and the discovery of it; for it was, and sometimes yet is, as much discoursed of in the north country, as anything that almost hath ever been heard of, and the relation printed, though now not to be gotten. I relate this with the greater confidence (though I may fail in some of the circumstances) because I saw and read the letter that was sent to Serjeant Hutton, who then lived at Goldsburgh in Yorkshire, from the judge before whom Walker and Mark Sharp were tried, and by whom they were condemned, and had a copy of it until about the year 1658, when I had it and many other books and papers taken from me; and this I confess to be one of the most convincing stories, being of undoubted verity, that ever I read, heard, or knew of, and carrieth with it the most evident force to make the most incredulous spirit to be satisfied that there are really, sometimes, such things as apparitions.—William Lumley."[1]

The above account, in which the object of the Spectral Appearance is obvious enough, is taken from the well-known "History of Durham," by that celebrated antiquarian the late Mr. Robert Surtees. It needs no comment, telling as it does so well, in quaint but plain language, its own remarkable story.

The next example to be recorded, the Apparition of the Rev. Mr. Naylor, may be found in Mr. John Nichols' "Literary Illustrations,"[2] and, though less startling than that already given, is certainly not without its own inherent interest :—

" Part of a Letter from Mr. Edward Walter, Fellow of S. John's College, Cambridge, to his friend in the country, dated 'Dec. 6, 1706.'

"'I should scarce have mentioned anything of the matter you write about of my own accord; but, since you have given yourself the trouble of an inquiry, I am, I think, obliged in friendship to relate all that I know of the matter; and that I do

---

[1] " History of Durham," by Robert Surtees, Esq.: under " Chester-le-Street." Vol. ii. pp. 147-148.

[2] " Nichols' Literary Illustrations." Vol. iv. p. 119, *et seq.* London, 1822.

the more willingly, because I can so soon produce my authority.

"'Mr. Shaw, to whom the apparition appeared, was Rector of Soldern, or Souldern, in Oxfordshire, late of S. John's College aforesaid; on whom Mr. Grove, his old Fellow Collegiate, called July last in his journey to the West, where he stayed a day or two, and promised to see him again on his return, which he did, and stayed three days with him; in that time one night after supper, Mr. Shaw told him that there happened a passage which he could not conceal from him, as being an intimate friend, and one to whom this transaction might have something more relation than another man. He proceeded therefore, and told him that about a week before that time, viz. July the 28th, 1706, as he was smoking and reading in his study about eleven or twelve at night, there came to him the apparition of Mr. Naylor, formerly Fellow of the said College, and dead some years ago, a friend of Mr. Shaw's, in the same garb he used to be in, with his hands clasped before him. Mr. Shaw, not being much surprised, asked him how he did and desired him to sit down, which Mr. Naylor did. They both sat there a considerable time and entertained one another with various discourses. Mr. Shaw then asked him after what manner they lived in the separate state; he answered, Far different from what they do here, but that he was very well. He inquired further, whether there was any of their old acquaintance in that place where he was? he answered, 'No, not one;' and then proceeded and told him that one of their old friends, naming Mr. Orchard, should die quickly, and he himself should not be long after. There was mention of several people's names; but who they were, or upon what occasion, Mr. Grove cannot or will not tell. Mr. Shaw then asked him whether he would not visit him again before that time; he answered, No, he could not; he had but three days allowed him, and farther he could not go. Mr. Shaw said, '*Fiat voluntas Domini;*' and the apparition left him. This is word for word as Mr. Shaw told Mr. Grove, and Mr. Grove told me.

"'*Note.*—What surprised Mr. Grove was, that as he had in his journey homewards occasion to ride through Clopton, or Claxton, he called upon one Mr. Clark, Fellow of our College aforesaid and curate there, when inquiring after College news, Mr. Clark told him Arthur Orchard[1] died that week, Aug. 7, 1706, which very much shocked Mr. Grove, and brought to his mind the story of Mr. Shaw afresh. About three weeks ago Mr. Shaw died of apoplexy in the desk, [*i.e.* when ministering in church,] of the same distemper poor Arthur Orchard died of.

"'*Note.*—Since this strange completion of matters, Mr. Grove has told this relation, and stands to the

---

[1] Arthur Orchard, of S. John's College, Cambridge, B.A. 1662; M.A. 1666; B.D. 1673.

truth of it; and that which confirms the narrative is, that he told the same to Dr. Baldiston, the present Vice-Chancellor and Master of Emanuel College, above a week before Mr. Shaw's death; and when he came to the College he was no way surprised as others were.

"'What farthers my belief of its being a true vision and not a dream, is Mr. Grove's incredulity of stories of this nature. Considering them both as men of learning and integrity, the one would not first have declared, nor the other have spread the same, were not the matter serious and real.

"'Edward Walter.'"

The following example of an Apparition in Scotland, unlike those already recorded, carries with it evidences of truth :—

"A gentleman of rank and property in Scotland served in his youth in the army of the Duke of York in Flanders. He occupied the same tent with two other officers, one of whom was sent on some service. One night during his absence, this gentleman while in bed saw the figure of his absent friend sitting on the vacant bed. He called to his companion, who also saw the figure, which spoke to them, and said he had just been killed at a certain place, pointing to his wound. He then requested them on returning to England, to call at a certain agent's house in a certain street, and to procure from him a document of great importance for the family of the deceased. If the agent, as was probable, should deny the possession of it, it would be found in a certain drawer of a cabinet in his room. Next day it appeared that the officer had been shot as he had told them, in the manner and at the time and place indicated. After the return of the troops to England, the two friends walking together one day, found themselves in the street where the agent lived, and the request of their friend recurred to both, they having hitherto forgotten it. They called on the agent, who denied having the paper in question; when they compelled him in their presence to open the drawer of the cabinet, where it was found and restored to the widow."[1]

An authentic record of the "Tyrone," or "Beresford Apparition," will now be given. It created a very great sensation at the time of its occurrence; and the narrative which follows has been pronounced traditionally "true and accurate" by a member of the family:—

"Lord Tyrone and Miss —— were born in Ireland, and were left orphans in their infancy to the care of the same person, by whom they were both educated in the principles of deism. Their guardian dying when they were each of them about fourteen years of age, they fell into very different hands.

"The persons on whom the care of them now devolved, used every means to eradicate the errone-

---

[1] "Letters on Animal Magnetism," by Dr. W. Gregory, p. 487. London, 1851.

ous principles they had imbibed, and to persuade them to embrace revealed religion, but in vain. Their arguments were strong enough to stagger their former faith. Though separated from each other, their friendship was unalterable, and they continued to regard each other with a sincere and fraternal affection.

"After some years were elapsed, and both were grown up, they made a solemn promise to each other that whichever should die first, would, if permitted, appear to the other, to declare what religion was most approved by the Supreme Being.

"Miss —— was shortly after addressed by Sir Martin Beresford, to whom she was after a few years married, but a change of condition had no power to alter their friendship. The families visited each other, and often spent some weeks together. A short time after one of these visits, Sir Martin remarked, that when his lady came down to breakfast, her countenance was disturbed, and inquired after her health. She assured him she was quite well. He then asked her if she had hurt her wrist: 'Have you sprained it?' said he, observing a black ribbon round it. She answered in the negative, and added, 'Let me conjure you, Sir Martin, never to inquire the cause of my wearing this ribbon; you will never see me without it. If it concerned you as a husband to know, I would not for a moment conceal it: I never in my life denied you a request, but of this I entreat you to forgive me the refusal, and never to urge me further on the subject.' 'Very well,' said he, smiling; 'since you beg me so earnestly, I will inquire no more.'

"The conversation here ended; but breakfast was scarcely over when Lady Beresford eagerly inquired if the post was come in; she was told it was not. In a few minutes she rang again and repeated the inquiry. She was again answered as at first. 'Do you expect letters?' said Sir Martin, 'that you are so anxious for the arrival of the post?' 'I do,' she answered, 'I expect to hear that Lord Tyrone is dead; he died last Tuesday at four o'clock.' 'I never in my life,' said Sir Martin, 'believed you superstitious; some idle dream has surely thus alarmed you.' At that instant the servant entered and delivered to them a letter sealed with black. 'It is as I expected,' exclaimed Lady Beresford, 'Lord Tyrone is dead.' Sir Martin opened the letter; it came from Lord Tyrone's steward, and contained the melancholy intelligence of his master's death, and on the very day and hour Lady Beresford had before specified. Sir Martin begged Lady Beresford to compose herself, and she assured him she felt much easier than she had done for a long time; and added, 'I can communicate intelligence to you which I know will prove welcome; I can assure you, beyond the possibility of a doubt, that I shall in some months present you with a son.' Sir Martin received this news with the greatest joy.

"After some months Lady Beresford was delivered of a son (she had before been the mother of only two daughters). Sir Martin survived the birth of his son little more than four years.

"After his decease his widow seldom left home; she visited no family but that of a clergyman who resided in the same village; with them she frequently passed a few hours; the rest of her time was spent in solitude, and she appeared determined for ever to banish all other society. The clergyman's family consisted of himself, his wife, and one son, who at the time of Sir Martin's death was quite a youth; to this son, however, she was after a few years married, notwithstanding the disparity of years and the manifest imprudence of a connexion so unequal in every point of view.

"Lady Beresford was treated by her young husband with contempt and cruelty, while at the same time his conduct evinced him the most abandoned libertine, utterly destitute of every principle of virtue and humanity. By this, her second husband, she had two daughters; after which such was the baseness of his conduct that she insisted on a separation. They parted for a few years, when so great was the contrition he expressed for his former conduct, that, won over by his supplications, promises, and entreaties, she was induced to pardon, and once more to reside with him, and was in time the mother of a son.

"The day on which she had lain-in a month being the anniversary of her birthday, she sent for Lady

Betty Cobb (of whose friendship she had long been possessed), and a few other friends, to request them to spend the day with her. About seven, the clergyman by whom she had been christened, and with whom she had all her life been intimate, came into the room to inquire after her health. She told him she was perfectly well, and requested him to spend the day with them; for, said she, 'This is my birthday. I am forty-eight to-day.' 'No, madam,' answered the clergyman, 'you are mistaken; your mother and myself have had many disputes concerning your age, and I have at last discovered that I was right. I happened to go last week into the parish where you were born; I was resolved to put an end to the dispute; I searched the register, and find that you are forty-seven this day.' 'You have signed my death warrant,' she exclaimed; 'I have then but a few hours to live. I must therefore entreat you to leave me immediately, as I have something of importance to settle before I die.'

"When the clergyman had left her, Lady Beresford sent to forbid the company coming, and at the same time to request Lady Betty Cobb and her son (of whom Sir Martin was the father, and who was then about twenty-two years of age), to come to her apartment immediately. Upon their arrival, having ordered the attendants to quit the room, 'I have something,' she said, 'of the greatest importance to communicate to you both before I die, a period which is not far distant. You, Lady Betty, are no stranger to the friendship which subsisted between Lord Tyrone and myself : we were educated under the same roof and in the same principles of deism. When the friends, into whose hands we afterwards fell, endeavoured to persuade us to embrace Revealed Religion, their arguments, though insufficient to convince, were powerful to stagger our former feelings, and to leave us wavering between the two opinions : in this perplexing state of doubt and uncertainty, we made a solemn promise to each other that whichever died first should (if permitted) appear to the other, and declare what religion was most acceptable to God; accordingly, one night, while Sir Martin and myself were in bed, I suddenly awoke and discovered Lord Tyrone sitting by my bedside. I screamed out and endeavoured to awake Sir Martin. "For Heaven's sake," I exclaimed, " Lord Tyrone, by what means or for what reason came you hither at this time of night?" " Have you then forgotten our promise ? " said he ; " I died last Tuesday at four o'clock, and have been permitted by the Supreme Being to appear to you to assure you that the Revealed Religion is true, and the only religion by which we can be saved. I am further suffered to inform you that you will soon produce a son, who it is decreed will marry my daughter; not many years after his birth Sir Martin will die, and you will marry again, and to a man by whose ill-treatment you will be rendered miserable : you will have two daughters and afterwards a son, in childbirth of whom you will die in the forty-seventh year of your age." "Just Heavens!" I exclaimed, "and cannot I prevent this?" "Undoubtedly," returned the spectre; "you are a free agent, and may prevent it all by resisting every temptation to a second marriage; but your passions are strong, you know not their power; hitherto you have had no trials. More I am not permitted to reveal, but if after this warning you persist in your infidelity, your lot in another world will be miserable indeed." "May I not ask," said I, "if you are happy?" "Had I been otherwise," he replied, "I should not have been permitted to appear to you." "I may, then, infer that you are happy?" He smiled. "But how," said I, "when morning comes, shall I know that your appearance to me has been real, and not the mere representation of my own imagination?" "Will not the news of my death be sufficient to convince you?" "No," I returned, "I might have had such a dream, and that dream accidentally come to pass. I will have some stronger proofs of its reality." "You shall," said he, and waving his hand, the bed curtains, which were crimson velvet, were instantly drawn through a large iron hoop by which the tester of the bed was suspended. "In that," said he, "you cannot be mistaken; no mortal arm could have performed this." "True," said I, "but sleeping we are often possessed of far more strength than when awake; though waking I could not have done it, asleep I might ; and I shall still doubt." "Here is a pocket-book ; in this," said he, "I will write my name ; you know my handwriting." I replied, "Yes." He wrote with a pencil on one side of the leaves. "Still," said I, "in the morning I may doubt ; though waking I could not imitate your hand, asleep I might." "You are hard of belief," said he. "Touch would injure you irreparably ; it is not for spirits to touch mortal flesh." "I do not," said I, "regard a slight blemish." "You are a woman of courage," said he, "hold out your hand." *I did; he struck my wrist: his hand was cold as marble ; in a moment the sinews shrunk up, every nerve withered.* "Now," said he, "while you live let no mortal eye behold that wrist : to see it is sacrilege." He stopped ; I turned to him again ; he was gone.

"'During the time I had conversed with him my thoughts were perfectly calm and collected ; but the moment he was gone I felt chilled with horror, the very bed moved under me. I endeavoured, but in vain, to awake Sir Martin ; all my attempts were ineffectual, and in this state of agitation and terror I lay for some time, when a shower of tears came to my relief and I fell asleep.

"'In the morning Sir Martin arose and dressed himself as usual, without perceiving the state the curtains remained in. When I awoke I found Sir Martin gone down; I arose, and having put on my clothes, went to the gallery adjoining the apartment and took from thence a long broom (such as cornices

are swept with); by the help of this I took down
with some difficulty the curtains, as I imagined
their extraordinary position might excite suspicion
in the family. I then went to the bureau, took up
my pocket-book, and bound a piece of black ribbon
round my wrist. When I came down, the agitation
of my mind had left an impression on my countenance too visible to pass unobserved by my
husband. He instantly remarked it, and asked the
cause; I informed him Lord Tyrone was no more,
that he died at the hour of four on the preceding
Tuesday, and desired him never to question me
more respecting the black ribbon, which he kindly
desisted from after. You, my son, as had been
foretold, I afterwards brought into the world, and in
little more than four years after your birth your
lamented father expired in my arms. After this
melancholy event I determined, as the only probable
chance to avoid the sequel of the prediction, for
ever to abandon all society, to give up every pleasure
resulting from it, and to pass the rest of my days
in solitude and retirement. But few can long
endure to exist in a state of perfect sequestration:
I began an intimacy with a family, and one alone;
nor could I foresee the fatal consequences which
afterwards resulted from it. Little did I think their
son, their only son, then a mere youth, would form
the person destined by fate to prove my destruction.
In a very few years I ceased to regard him with
indifference; I endeavoured by every possible way

to conquer a passion, the fatal effects of which I too well knew. I had fondly imagined I had overcome its influence, when the evening of one fatal day terminated my fortitude and plunged me in a moment down that abyss I had so long been meditating how to shun. He had often solicited his parents for leave to go into the army, and at last obtained permission, and came to bid me adieu before his departure. The instant he entered the room he fell upon his knees at my feet, told me he was miserable, and that I alone was the cause. At that moment my fortitude forsook me, I gave myself up as lost, and regarding my fate as inevitable, without further hesitation consented to a union, the immediate result of which I knew to be misery, and its end death. The conduct of my husband after a few years amply justified a separation, and I hoped by these means to avoid the fatal sequel of the prophecy: but won over by his reiterated entreaties, I was prevailed upon to pardon and once more reside with him, though not till after I had, as I thought, passed my forty-seventh year.

"' But alas! I have this day heard from indisputable authority that I have hitherto lain under a mistake with regard to my age, and that I am but forty-seven to-day. Of the near approach of my death then I entertain not the slightest doubt; but I do not dread its arrival; armed with the sacred precepts of Christianity I can meet the King of Terrors without dismay, and without fear bid adieu to mortality for ever.

"'When I am dead, as the necessity for concealment closes with my life, I could wish that you, Lady Betty, would unbind my wrist, take from thence the black ribbon, and let my son with yourself behold it.' Lady Beresford here paused for some time, but resuming the conversation she entreated her son would behave himself so as to merit the high honour he would in future receive from a union with the daughter of Lord Tyrone.

"Lady B. then expressed a wish to lay down on the bed and endeavour to compose herself to sleep. Lady Betty Cobb and her son immediately called her domestics and quitted the room, having first desired them to watch their mistress attentively, and if they observed the smallest change in her, to call instantly.

"An hour passed and all was quiet in the room. They listened at the door and everything remained still, but in half an hour more a bell rang violently; they flew to her apartment, but before they reached the door, they heard the servants exclaim, 'Oh, she is dead!' Lady Betty then bade the servants for a few minutes to quit the room, and herself with Lady Beresford's son approached the bed of his mother; they knelt down by the side of it; Lady Betty lifted up her hand and untied the ribbon,— *the wrist was found exactly as Lady Beresford had described it, every sinew shrunk, every nerve withered.*

"Lady Beresford's son, as had been predicted, is

since married to Lord Tyrone's daughter. The black ribbon and pocket-book were formerly in the possession of Lady Betty Cobb, Marlborough Buildings, Bath, who, during her long life, was ever ready to attest the truth of this narration, as are, to the present hour, the whole of the Tyrone and Beresford families."[1]

Three remarkable examples of Spectral Appearances must now be given, because of their inherent interest and corresponding likeness. The first is recorded by Glanville, a learned and pious author already referred to; the second is the case of Dr. Ferrar, and the third that of the "Wynyard Ghost Story."

(I.) Glanville tells a story regarding the appearance of a spirit in fulfilment of a promise made during lifetime, which is full of point and purpose. It runs thus. The substance, not the exact words, of the narrative are here given :—In the seventeenth century there lived two friends, Major George Sydenham of Dulverton in the county of Somerset, and Captain William Dyke of the same county. They were both reputed to be unbelievers in the Christian religion, if not avowed atheists. During the

---

[1] A member of the noble family of Beresford thus wrote (A.D. 1873) to a friend of the Editor, with reference to the above narrative :—" The tradition in our family is entirely in favour of the truth of the Spectral Appearance, and the account which I have read, and return, is in my opinion a true and faithful narration of it."

civil wars they had each served under the Parliamentary generals, and took an active part on the side of the rebels.

Having held many discussions both on the subject of religion and irreligion, they eventually argued out the fact of the immortality of the soul, which each felt disposed to deny: and finally they agreed between themselves that whichever of them died first, should (if such a possibility existed,) appear on the third day after death to the survivor in Major Sydenham's summer-house at Dulverton, and enlighten him as to the existence of a future state of rewards and punishments.

In due course Major Sydenham died; and Captain Dyke, in company with a cousin of his own, a celebrated physician, who was attending a sick child at Major Sydenham's house, but who knew nothing of the matter in hand, arrived there. Captain Dyke and his relative Dr. Dyke, the physician, occupied the same bedroom. The latter was surprised to hear the captain ask of the servant for two of the largest candles that could be obtained, and sought an explanation. The captain then informed him of his promise to Major Sydenham, and of his own determined resolution to fulfil it. Dr. Dyke urged with considerable force that as there was no warrant for making such engagements, they were to be regarded as unquestionably wrong; and pointed out, firstly, that evil spirits might take advantage of the situation, and secondly, that such a tempting of the Almighty was altogether wrong.

"This may be all very true," responded Captain Dyke, "but as I faithfully promised to go, go I will. If you will come and sit up with me, well and good: and I shall be grateful. But if not, I shall certainly go alone."

Then, placing his watch on the table, he waited until half-past eleven; when taking up the candles, he walked up and down in close proximity to the entrance of the summer-house, until two o'clock, without either seeing or hearing anything extraordinary.

Upon this he formed two conclusions; either that the soul perished with the body, or that the laws of the spiritual world forbade his friend Major Sydenham abiding by his pledge.

Six weeks afterwards, however, Captain Dyke and his relation the physician had occasion to go to Eton, where one of the sons of the former was to be placed at the college. They lodged at the S. Christopher's Inn, occupying different sleeping-rooms. On the last morning of their stay, Captain Dyke was unusually late, and when he entered the doctor's room was like a man struck with madness, his eyes staring, his knees refusing to support him, and his whole appearance altered.

"What is the matter?" asked Dr. Dyke.

"I have seen the major," replied the captain; "for if ever I saw him in my life, I certainly saw him just now."

Upon the doctor pressing for details, Captain Dyke gave the following account:—"After it was first light this morning, someone pulled back the curtains of my bed suddenly, and I saw the major exactly as I had seen him in life. 'I could not,' he said, 'come at the time appointed, but I am here now to tell you that there is a God, a very just and terrible God, and that if you do not turn over a new leaf you will find it so.' He then disappeared."

It is said, finally, that Captain Dyke's truthfulness was so notorious, as to preclude the possibility of doubting his relation of the occurrence. Furthermore, the apparition and warnings of his departed friend exercised a visible effect on his character and life, which latter was prolonged for two years; during which period he is said to have had the words then spoken to him always sounding in his ears.

(II.) The celebrated Nicholas Ferrar, of Little Gidding, (who, in the seventeenth century, lived a most retired, religious, and pious life,) had a brother, a physician in London. This physician made a compact with his eldest and favourite daughter that whichever of them died first should, if happy, appear to the other. This compact is said to have proved the subject of many conversations and religious discussions between father and child. The latter is reported to have been very averse to making any such agreement; but being overcome by arguments as to the reasonableness of such a course (if permitted by a gracious and merciful God) at last consented. After this she married and settled with her husband at Gillingham Lodge, in the county of Wiltshire. Here she was prematurely confined; and during her illness, one night by mistake took poison, and died quite suddenly. That very night her spirit appeared to her father in London, the curtains of whose bed she drew back, and with a sweet but mournful expression looked upon him, and then gradually faded away. In fact, and as a test of the objective reality of his daughter's apparition, Dr. Ferrar, deeply impressed by the occurrence, announced the death of his daughter to his family two days before he received intelligence of it by the then tardy post.

(III.) John Cope Sherbroke and George Wynyard appear in the "Army List" of 1785, the one as a captain and the other lieutenant in the 33rd Regiment,—a corps which some years after had the honour to be commanded by the Hon. Arthur Wellesley, subsequently Duke of Wellington. The regiment was then on service in Canada, and Sherbroke and Wynyard, being of congenial tastes, had become great friends. It was their custom to spend in study much of the time which their brother officers devoted to idle pleasures. According to a narration[1] resting on the best authority now attain-

---

[1] The record of this came to the Editor, through a friend, from the late Rev. W. Hastings Kelke, M.A., sometime Rector of Drayton Beauchamp, in the county of Bucks.

able, they were one afternoon sitting in Wynyard's apartment. It was perfectly light, the hour was about four o'clock: they had dined, but neither of them had drunk wine, and they had retired from their mess to continue together the occupations of the morning. It ought to have been said that the apartment in which they were had two doors in it, the one opening into a passage and the other leading into Wynyard's bedroom. There was no other means of entering the sitting-room, so that any person passing into the bedroom must have remained there unless he returned by the way he entered. This point is of consequence to the story.

"As these two young officers were pursuing their studies, Sherbroke, whose eyes happened accidentally to glance from the book before him towards the door which opened to the passage, all at once observed a tall youth of about twenty years of age whose appearance was that of extreme emaciation. Struck with the presence of a perfect stranger, he immediately turned to his friend, who was sitting near him, and directed his attention to the guest who had thus strangely broken in upon their studies. As soon as Wynyard's eyes were turned towards the mysterious visitor his countenance became suddenly agitated. 'I have heard,' says Sir John Sherbroke, 'of a man's being as pale as death, but I never saw a living face assume the appearance of a corpse except Wynyard's at that moment.' As they looked silently at the form before them (for

Wynyard, who seemed to apprehend the import of the appearance, was deprived of the faculty of speech, and Sherbroke, perceiving the agitation of his friend, felt no inclination to address it—as they looked silently upon the figure it proceeded slowly into the adjoining apartment, and in the act of passing them cast its eyes with an expression of somewhat melancholy affection on young Wynyard. The oppression of this extraordinary presence was no sooner removed than Wynyard, seizing his friend by the arm, and drawing a deep breath as if recovering from the suffocation of intense astonishment and emotion, muttered in a low and almost inaudible tone of voice, 'Great God, my brother!' 'Your brother!' repeated Sherbroke, 'what can you mean? Wynyard, there must be some deception; follow me;' and immediately taking his friend by the arm, he preceded him into the bedroom, which, as before stated, was connected with the sitting-room, and into which the strange visitor had evidently entered. It has already been said that from this chamber there was no possibility of withdrawing but by the way of the apartment, through which the figure had certainly never returned. Imagine then the astonishment of the young officers when, on finding themselves in the chamber, they perceived that the room was perfectly untenanted. Wynyard's mind had received an impression at the first moment of his observing him, that the figure whom he had seen was the spirit of his brother. Sherbroke still persevered in strenuously believing that some delusion had been practised. They took note of the day and hour in which the event had happened, but they resolved not to mention the occurrence in the regiment, and gradually they persuaded each other that they had been imposed upon by some artifice of their fellow-officers, though they could neither account for the means of its execution. They were content to imagine anything possible rather than admit the possibility of a supernatural appearance. But though they had attempted these stratagems of self-delusion, Wynyard could not help expressing his solicitude with respect to the safety of the brother whose apparition he had either seen or imagined himself to have seen; and the anxiety which he exhibited for letters from England, and his frequent mention of his brother's health, at length awakened the curiosity of his comrades, and eventually betrayed him into a declaration of the circumstances which he had in vain determined to conceal. The story of the silent and unbidden visitor was no sooner bruited abroad than the arrival of Wynyard's letters from England were welcomed with more than usual eagerness, for they promised to afford the clue to the mystery which had happened among themselves.

"By the first ships no intelligence relating to the story could have been received, for they had all departed from England previously to the appearance of the spirit. At length, the long wished-for vessel arrived; all the officers had letters except Wynyard. They examined the several newspapers, but they contained no mention of any death or of any other circumstance connected with his family that could account for the preternatural event. There was a solitary letter for Sherbroke still unopened. The officers had received their letters in the mess-room at the hour of supper. After Sherbroke had broken the seal of his last packet, and cast a glance on its contents, he beckoned his friend away from the company, and departed from the room. All were silent. The suspense of the interest was now at its climax; the impatience for the return of Sherbroke was inexpressible. They doubted not but that letter had contained the long-expected intelligence.

"After the interval of an hour, Sherbroke joined them. No one dared inquire the nature of his correspondence; but they waited in mute attention, expecting that he would himself touch upon the subject. His mind was manifestly full of thoughts that pained, bewildered, and oppressed him. He drew near to the fire-place, and leaning his head on the mantlepiece, after a pause of some moments, said in a low voice to the person who was nearest him, Wynyard's brother was dead. 'Dear John, break to your friend Wynyard the death of his favourite brother.' *He had died on the day and at the very hour on which the friends had seen his spirit pass so mysteriously through the apartment.*

"It might have been imagined that these events would have been sufficient to have impressed the mind of Sherbroke with the conviction of their truth, but so strong was his prepossession against the existence or even the possibility of any preternatural intercourse with the spirits of the departed, that he still entertained a doubt of the report of his senses, supported as their testimony was by the coincidence of sight and event. Some years after, on his return to England, he was with two gentlemen in Piccadilly, when on the opposite side of the street he saw a person bearing the most striking resemblance to the figure which had been disclosed to Wynyard and himself. His companions were acquainted with the story, and he instantly directed their attention to the gentleman opposite, as the individual who had contrived to enter and depart from Wynyard's apartment without their being conscious of the means.

"Full of this impression, he immediately went over and addressed the gentleman. He now fully expected to elucidate the mystery. He apologized for the interruption, but excused it by relating the occurrence which had induced him to the commission of this solecism in manners. The gentleman received him as a friend. He had never been out of the country, but he was the twin brother of the youth whose spirit had been seen.

"From the interesting character of this narration— the facts of the vision occurring in daylight, and to two persons ; and of the subsequent verification of likeness by the party not previously acquainted with the subject of the vision, it is much to be regretted that no direct report of particulars had come to us. There is all other desirable authentication for the story, and sufficient evidence to prove that the two gentlemen believed and often told nearly what is here reported.

"Dr. Mayo makes the following statement on the subject: 'I have had opportunities of inquiring of two near relations of this General Wynyard, upon what evidence the above story rests. They told me that they had each heard it from his own mouth. More recently a gentleman, whose accuracy of recollection exceeds that of most people, had told me that he had heard the late Sir John Sherbroke, the other party in the ghost story, tell it in much the same way at the dinner-table. A writer in 'Notes and Queries' for July 3, 1858, states that the brother, not twin-brother, whose spirit appeared to Wynyard and his friend, was John Otway Wynyard, Lieutenant in the 3rd Regiment of Foot-guards, who died on the 15th of October, 1785. As this gentleman writes with a minute knowledge of the family history, this date may be considered as that of the alleged spiritual incident.

"In 'Notes and Queries' for July 2nd, 1859, appeared a correspondence, giving the strongest testimony then attainable to the truth of the Wynyard ghost story. A series of queries on the subject being drawn up at Quebec, by Sir John Harvey, Adjutant-General of the forces in Canada, was sent to Colonel Gore of the same garrison, who was understood to be a survivor of the officers who were with Sherbroke and Wynyard at the time of the occurrence, and Colonel Gore explicitly replied to the following effect: He was present at Sydney, in the island of Cape Breton, in the autumn of 1785 or 1786, when the incident happened. It was in the then new barrack, and the place was blocked up by ice so as to have no communication with any part of the world. He was one of the first persons who entered the room after the apparition was seen. The ghost passed them as they were sitting at coffee, between eight and nine in the evening, and went into G. Wynyard's bed closet, the window of which was putt[i]ed down. He next day suggested to Sherbroke the propriety of making a memorandum of the incident, which was done. 'I remember the date, and on the 6th of June our first letters from England brought the news of John Wynyard's death, [which had happened] on the very night they saw his apparition.' Colonel Gore was under the impression that the person afterwards seen in one of the streets of London, by Sherbroke and William Wynyard, was not a brother of the latter family, but a gentleman named (he thought) Hayman, noted for being like the deceased John Wynyard, and who affected to dress like him."

So much for these records and testimonies. The following, now to be narrated, not altogether unlike them, and producing a good result on the person who witnessed the apparition, is of almost equal interest:—

"Lord Chedworth[1] had living with him the orphan daughter of a sister of his, a Miss Wright, who often related this circumstance: Lord Chedworth was a good man, and seemed anxious to do his duty, but, unfortunately, he had considerable intellectual doubts as to the existence of the soul in another world. He had a great friendship for a gentleman, whom he had known from his boyhood, and who was, like himself, one of those unbelieving mortals that must have ocular demonstration for everything. They often met, and often, too, renewed the subject so interesting to both; but neither could help the other to that happy conviction which was honestly wished for by each.

"One morning Miss Wright observed on her uncle joining her at breakfast, a considerable gloom of thought and trouble displayed on his countenance.

---

[1] The barony of Chedworth was conferred upon John Howe, Esq., of Chedworth, co. Gloucester, on May 12, 1741. He had two sons, John Thynne, the nobleman referred to in the above account, and Henry Frederick, who in turn succeeded him in the title. His daughter Mary married Alexander Wright, Esq., whose daughter Mary Wright is the lady mentioned in the above narrative. Miss Wright's cousin John inherited as fourth baron, but died unmarried, Oct. 29, 1804, when the peerage became extinct.

He ate little, and was unusually silent. At last, he said, 'Molly' (for thus he familiarly called her), 'I had a strange visitor last night. My old friend B—— came to me.'

"'How?' said Miss Wright, 'did he come after I went to bed?'

"'His spirit did,' said Lord Chedworth, solemnly.

"'Oh! my dear uncle, how could the spirit of a living man appear?' said she, smiling.

"'He is dead, beyond doubt,' replied his lordship; 'listen, and then laugh as much as you please. I had not entered my bedroom many minutes when he stood before me. Like you, I could not but think that I was looking on the living man, and so accosted him; but he answered, "Chedworth, I died this night at eight o'clock; I come to tell you, that there is another world beyond the grave; and that there is a righteous God Who judgeth all."'

"'Depend upon it, uncle, it was only a dream!' But while Miss Wright was thus speaking a groom on horseback rode up the avenue, and immediately after delivered a letter to Lord Chedworth, announcing the sudden death of his friend. Whatever construction the reader may be disposed to put upon this narrative, it is not unimportant to add that the effect upon the mind of Lord Chedworth was as happy as it was permanent. All his doubts were at once removed, and for ever."

The well-known Lyttelton Ghost Story may now be fitly recorded. It created a great and widespread interest at the time of its occurrence, and was criticised and commented upon by many. Several versions of it have already appeared in print, and they seem to vary in certain unimportant details. The Editor, instead of writing out what has already appeared, prefers to set forth at length various documents containing independent evidence of the truth of the several apparitions, which by the courtesy and kindness of the present accomplished bearer of the title, he is enabled to embody *verbatim* in this volume, having been permitted to transcribe them from the originals in Lord Lyttelton's possession.

The subject of this narrative was the son of George, Lord Lyttelton, who was alike distinguished for the raciness of his wit and the profligacy of his manners. The latter trait of his character has induced many persons to suppose the apparition which he asserted he had seen, to have been the effect of a conscience quickened with remorse and misgivings, on account of many vices. The probability of the narrative[1] has, consequently, been much

---

[1] Another narrative of this remarkable event, which substantially corresponds with those given in the text above is provided here. In certain respects there are discrepancies, and just those kinds of discrepancies which might reasonably have been looked for in accounts drawn up by different hands; but in the main facts, regarding which there can be no reasonable doubt, there is a remarkable and notable identity in all the leading features: "Two nights before, on

questioned; but two gentlemen, one of whom was at Pitt Place, the seat of Lord Lyttelton, and the other in the immediate neighbourhood, at the time of his lordship's death, bore ample testimony to the veracity of the whole affair. The several narratives of the singular occurrence correspond in material points; and the following are the circumstantial particulars written by the gentleman who was at the time on a visit to his lordship:—

"I was at Pitt Place, Epsom, when Lord Lyttelton died; Lord Fortescue, Mrs. Flood, and the two Miss Amphletts were also present. Lord Lyttelton had not long been returned from Ireland, and frequently had been seized with suffocating fits; he was attacked several times by them in the course of the preceding month, while he was at his house in Hill Street, Berkeley Square. It happened that he dreamt, three days before his death, that he saw a fluttering bird, and afterwards a woman appeared to him in white apparel and said to him, 'Prepare to die, you will not exist three days!' His lordship was much alarmed, and called to a servant

---

Lord Lyttelton retiring to bed, after his servant was dismissed and his light extinguished, he had heard a noise resembling the fluttering of a dove at his chamber window. This attracted his attention to the spot; when, looking in the direction of the sound, he saw the figure of an unhappy female whom he had seduced, and who, when deserted, had put a violent end to her own existence, standing in the aperture of the window from which the fluttering sound had proceeded. The

from a closet adjoining, who found him much agitated and in a profuse perspiration; the circumstance had a considerable effect all the next day on his lordship's spirits. On the third day, while his lordship was at breakfast with the above personages, he said, 'If I live over to-night I shall have jockied the ghost, for this is the third day.' The whole party presently set off for Pitt Place, where they had not long arrived before his lordship was visited by one of his accustomed fits. After a short interval he recovered. He dined at five o'clock that day, and went to bed at eleven, when his servant was about to give him rhubarb and mint-water, but his lordship perceiving him stir it with a toothpick, called him a slovenly dog, and bade him go and fetch a teaspoon; but on the man's return he found his Master in a fit, and the

---

form approached the foot of the bed, the room was preternaturally light, the objects of the chamber were distinctly visible. Raising her hand and pointing to a dial which stood on the mantlepiece of the chimney, the figure, with a severe solemnity of voice and manner, answered to the appalled and conscience-stricken man that at that very hour, on the third day after the visitation, his life and his sins would be concluded, and nothing but their punishment remain, if he availed himself not of the warning to repentance which he had thus received. The eye of Lord Lyttelton glanced upon the dial; the hand was on the stroke of twelve: again the apartment was involved in total darkness—the warning spirit disappeared, and bore away at her departure all the lightness of heart and buoyancy of spirit, ready flow of wit, and vivacity of manner, which had formerly been the pride and ornament

pillow being placed high, his chin bore hard upon his neck, when the servant, instead of relieving his master on the instant from his perilous situation, ran in his fright and called out for help, but on his return he found his lordship dead.

"In explanation of this strange tale it is said that Lord Lyttelton acknowledged, previously to his death, that the woman he had seen in his dream was the 'mother' of the two Misses Amphletts mentioned above, whom, together with a third sister then in Ireland, his lordship had seduced and prevailed on to leave their parent, who resided near his country residence in Shropshire. It is further stated that Mrs. Amphlett died of grief through the desertion of her children at the precise time when the female vision appeared to his lordship. The most surprising part of the story, because the

---

of the unhappy being to whom she had delivered her tremendous summons. Such was the tale that Lord Lyttelton delivered to his companions. They laughed at his superstition, and endeavoured to convince him that his mind must have been impressed with this idea by some dream of a more consistent nature than dreams generally are, and that he had mistaken the visions of his sleep for the visitation of a spirit. He was consoled, but not convinced; he felt relieved by their distrust, and on the second night after the appearance of the spectre, he retreated to his apartment with his faith in the reality of the transaction somewhat shaken; and his spirits, though not revived, certainly lightened of somewhat of their oppression. On the succeeding day the guests of Lord Lyttelton, with the connivance of his attendant, had provided that the clocks throughout the house should be advanced an

most difficult of explanation, yet remains to be related. On the second day Miles Peter Andrews, one of Lord Lyttelton's most intimate friends, left the dinner-party at an early hour, being called away upon business to Dartford, where he was the owner of certain powder-mills. He had all along professed himself one of the most determined sceptics as to the vision, and therefore ceased to think of it. On the third night, however, when he had been in bed about half an hour, and still remained, as he imagined, wide awake, his curtains were suddenly pulled aside, and Lord Lyttelton appeared before him in his robe-de-chambre and night-cap. Mr. Andrews gazed at his visitor for some time in silent wonder, and then began to reproach him for so odd a freak in coming down to Dartford Mills without any previous notice, as he

---

hour; by occupying the host's attention during the whole day with different and successive objects of amusement, they contributed to prevent his discovering the imposture. Ten o'clock struck: the nobleman was silent and depressed. Eleven struck, the depression deepened, and now not even a smile, or the slightest movement of his eye indicated him to be conscious of the efforts of his associates, as they attempted to dispel his gloom. Twelve struck. 'Thank God! I am safe,' exclaimed Lord Lyttelton, 'the ghost was a liar after all. Some wine, there. Congratulate me, my friends; congratulate me on my reprieve. Why, what a fool I was to be cast down by so idle and absurd a circumstance! But, however, it is time for bed. We'll be up early and out with the hounds to-morrow. By my faith, it's half-past twelve, so good night!' and he returned to his chamber convinced of his

hardly knew how on the emergency to find his lordship the requisite accommodation. 'Nevertheless,' said Andrews, 'I will get up and see what can be done for you.' With this view he turned aside to ring the bell; but on looking round again he could see no signs of his strange visitor. Soon afterwards the bell was rung for his servant, and upon his asking what had become of Lord Lyttelton, the man, evidently much surprised at the question, replied that he had seen nothing of him since they had left Pitt Place. 'Psha, you fool,' exclaimed Mr. Andrews, 'he was here this moment at my bedside.' The servant, more astonished than ever, declared that he did not well understand how that could be, since he must have seen him enter; whereupon Mr. Andrews rose, and having dressed himself, searched the house and grounds, but Lord

security, and believing that the threatened hour of peril was now past. His guests remained together to await the completion of the time so ominously designated by the vision. A quarter of an hour had elapsed: they heard the valet descend from his master's room. It was just twelve. Lord Lyttelton's bell rang violently. The company ran in a body to his apartment. The clock struck one at their entrance, the unhappy nobleman lay extended on the bed before them, pale and lifeless, and his countenance terribly convulsed."

In his "Memoirs," Sir Nathaniel Wraxall has the following relating to this occurrence:—

"Dining at Pitt Place, about four years after the death of Lord Lyttelton, in the year 1783, I had the curiosity to visit the bed-chamber, where the casement window, at which Lord Lyttelton asserted the dove appeared to flutter, was pointed

Lyttelton was nowhere to be found. Still, he could not help believing that his friend, who was fond of practical jokes, had played him this trick for his previously expressed scepticism in the matter of the dream. But he soon viewed the whole affair in a different light. About four o'clock on the same day an express arrived from a friend with the news of Lord Lyttelton's death, and the whole manner of it, as related by the valet to those who were in the house at the time. In Mr. Andrews's subsequent visits to Pitt Place, no solicitations could ever induce him to sleep there; he would invariably return, however late, to the Spread Eagle Inn, at Epsom, for the night."

Remarkable Dream of Thomas, Lord Lyttelton.[1]

" On Thursday, the 25th of November, 1779, out to me; and at his stepmother's, the Dowager Lady Lyttelton's in Portugal Street, Grosvenor Square, who being a woman of very lively imagination, lent an implicit faith to all the supernatural facts which were supposed to have accompanied or produced Lord Lyttelton's end. I have frequently seen a painting which she herself executed in 1780, especially to commemorate the event: it hung in a conspicuous part of her drawing-room. There the dove appears at the window, while a female figure, habited in white, stands at the foot of the bed, announcing to Lord Lyttelton his dissolution. Every part of the picture was faithfully designed after the description given to her by the valet-de-chambre who attended him, to whom his master related all the circumstances."

[1] Copied from a paper in the autograph of Lord Westcote,

Thomas, Lord Lyttelton, when he came to breakfast, declared to Mrs. Flood, wife of Frederick Flood, Esq., of the kingdom of Ireland, and to the three Miss Amphletts, who were lodged in his house in Hill Street, London (where he then also was), that he had had an extraordinary dream the night before. He said he thought he was in a room which a bird flew into, which appearance was suddenly changed into that of a woman dressed in white, who bade him prepare to die. To which he answered, 'I hope not soon, not in two months.' She replied, 'Yes, in three days.' He said he did not much regard it, because he could in some measure account for it; for that a few days before he had been with Mrs. Dawson when a robin-redbreast flew into her room.

"When he had dressed himself that day to go to the House of Lords, he said he thought he did not look as if he was likely to die. In the evening of

---

entitled " Remarkable Circumstances attending the Death of Thomas, Lord Lyttelton," which the present Lord Lyttelton most courteously entrusted to the Editor of this volume, together with several other original documents relating to the same, as follows :—1. Extract from Mr. Plumer Ward's "Illustrations of Human Life," vol. i. p. 165. 2. Written account given by Sir Digby Neave, bart., to Lord Lyttelton in 1860. 3. MS. containing Mr. George Fortescue's testimony, signed S. L. 4. The following declaration :—" Chiswick, May 6th, 1867. Miles Peter Andrews told me the story of Lord Lyttelton's appearance to him, driving with me at Wingerworth, many years ago.—Anna Hunloke."

the following day, being Friday, he told the eldest Miss Amphlett that she looked melancholy; but, said he, 'You are foolish and fearful. I have lived two days, and, God willing, I will live out the third.'

"On the morning of Saturday he told the same ladies that he was very well, and believed he should bilk the ghost. Some hours afterwards he went with them, Mr. Fortescue, and Captain Wolseley, to Pitt Place, at Epsom; withdrew to his bed-chamber soon after eleven o'clock at night, talked cheerfully to his servant, and particularly inquired of him what care had been taken to provide good rolls for his breakfast the next morning, stepped into his bed with his waistcoat on, and as his servant was pulling it off, put his hand to his side, sunk back and immediately expired without a groan. He ate a good dinner after his arrival at Pitt Place, took an egg for his supper, and did not seem to be at all out of order, except that while he was eating his soup at dinner he had a rising in his throat, a thing which had often happened to him before, and which obliged him to spit some of it out. His physician, Dr. Fothergill, told me Lord Lyttelton had in the summer preceding a bad pain in his side, and he judged that some gut vessel in the part where he felt the pain gave way, and to that he conjectured his death was owing. His declaration of his dream and his expressions above mentioned, consequential thereon, were upon a close inquiry asserted to me to have been so, by Mrs. Flood, the eldest Miss Amphlett, Captain Wolseley, and his valet-de-chambre Faulkner,[1] who dressed him on the Thursday; and the manner of his death was related to me by William Stuckey, in the presence of Mr. Fortescue and Captain Wolseley, Stuckey being the servant who attended him in his bed-chamber, and in whose arms he died.

"Westcote.[2]

" February the 13th, 1780."

Lord Lyttelton is also asserted to have appeared

---

[1] Lord Lyttelton's valet made the following statement :—
" That Lord Lyttelton made his usual preparations for bed; that he kept every now and then looking for his watch; that when he got into bed, he ordered his curtains to be closed at the foot. It was now within a minute or two of twelve by his watch; he asked to look at mine, and seemed pleased to find it nearly keep time with his own. His lordship then put them both to his ear, to satisfy himself if they went. When it was more than a quarter after twelve by our watches, he said, ' This mysterious lady is not a true prophetess, I find.' When it was near the real hour of twelve, he said, ' Come, I'll wait no longer; get me my medicine, I'll take it, and try to sleep.' I just stepped into the dressing-room to prepare the physic, and had mixed it, when I thought I heard my lord breathing very hard. I ran to him, and found him in the agonies of death."—" Gentleman's Magazine," vol. lxxxv. part i. p. 598, A.D. 1815.

[2] In Boswell's " Life of Samuel Johnson " (vol. iv. p. 313) the Doctor is recorded to have said, " It is the most extraordinary occurrence in my days. I heard it from Lord Westcote, his uncle. I am so glad to have evidence of the spiritual world, that I am willing to believe it."

to Mr. Andrews, his friend and boon companion, at the time of his lordship's sudden and mysterious death. Of this fact testimony is furnished by Mr. Plumer Ward, M.P., in his "Illustrations of Human Life," from which (vol. i. p. 165) the following narrative is taken :—

"I had often heard much and read much of Lord Lyttelton's seeing a ghost before his death, and of himself as a ghost appearing to Mr. Andrews; and one evening, sitting near that gentleman, during a pause in the debates in the House of Commons, I ventured to ask him whether there was any and what truth in the detailed story so confidently related. Mr. Andrews, as perhaps I ought to have expected, did not much like the conversation. He looked grave and uneasy, and I asked pardon for my impertinent curiosity. Upon this he good-naturedly said, 'It is not a subject I am fond of, and least of all in such a place as this; but if you will come and dine with me, I will tell you what is true and what is false.' I gladly accepted the proposal, and I think my recollection is perfect as to the following narrative :—'Mr. Andrews in his youth was the boon-companion, not to say fellow-rake, of Lord Lyttelton, who, as is well known, was a man distinguished for abilities, but also for a profligacy of morals which few could equal. With all this he was remarkable for what may be called unnatural cowardice in one so determinedly wicked. He never repented, yet could never stifle his conscience. He

never could allow, yet never could deny, a world to come, and he contemplated with unceasing terror what would probably be his own state in such a world if there was one. He was always melancholy with fear, or mad in defiance; and probably his principal misery here was, that with all his endeavours, he never could extinguish the dread of an hereafter . . . .
Andrews was at his house at Dartford when Lord Lyttelton died at Pitt Place, Epsom, thirty miles off. Andrews' house was full of company, and he expected Lord Lyttelton, whom he had left in his usual state of health, to join them the next day, which was Sunday. Andrews himself feeling much indisposed on the Saturday evening, retired early to bed, and requested Mrs. Pigou, one of his guests, to do the honours of the supper-table. He admitted that, when in bed, he fell into a feverish sleep, but was waked between eleven and twelve by somebody opening his curtains. It was Lord Lyttelton in a night-gown and cap, which Andrews recognized. He also plainly spoke to him, saying he was come to tell him all was over. The world said he informed him there was another state, and bade him repent, &c. That was not so. And I confine myself to the exact words of this relation.

"'Now it seems that Lord Lyttelton was fond of horse-play, or what we should call *mauvaise plaisanterie;* and, having often made Andrews the subject of it, the latter had threatened him with manual chastisement next time it occurred. On the present occasion, thinking this annoyance renewed, he threw the first thing he could find, which were his slippers, at Lord Lyttelton's head. The figure retreated towards a dressing-room which had no ingress or egress except through the bed-chamber, and Andrews, very angry, leapt out of bed, to follow it into the dressing-room. It was not there. Surprised, he returned to the bedroom, which he strictly searched. The door was locked on the inside, yet no Lord Lyttelton was to be found. He was astonished, but not alarmed, so convinced was he that it was some trick of Lord Lyttelton, who, he supposed, had arrived, according to his engagement, but after he, Andrews, had retired. He therefore rang for his servant, and asked if Lord Lyttelton was not come. The man said, "No." "You may depend upon it," replied he, out of humour, "he is somewhere in the house, for he was here just now, and is playing some trick." But how he could have got into the bedroom with the door locked puzzled both master and man. Convinced, however, that he was somewhere in the house, Andrews, in his anger, ordered that no bed should be given him, saying he might go to an inn, or sleep in the stables. Be that as it may, he never appeared again, and Andrews went to sleep.

"'It happened that Mrs. Pigou was to go to town early the next morning. What was her astonishment, having heard the disturbance of the night before, to hear on her arrival about nine o'clock that

Lord Lyttelton had died the very night he was supposed to have been seen. She immediately sent an express to Dartford with the news; upon the receipt of which, Andrews, (quite well, and remembering accurately all that had passed,) swooned away. He could not understand it, but it had a most serious effect upon him, so that—to use his own expression —he "was not his own man again for three years."'

"Such is the celebrated story; stript of its ornamentations and exaggerations; and for one, I own, if not convinced that this was a real message from Heaven, which certainly I am not, I at least think the hand of Providence was seen in it; working upon the imagination, if you please, and therefore suspending no law of Nature (though that after all is an ambiguous term), but still Providence, in a character not to be mistaken."

The following remarkable occurrence of the Spectral Appearances of two persons, one recently dead and the other a canonized saint of the Roman Catholic Church, which occurred about thirty years ago, is now published for the first time. It is known as "The Weld Ghost Story:"—

"Philip Weld was a younger son of Mr. James Weld of Archer's Lodge, near Southampton, and a nephew of the late Cardinal Weld, the head of that ancient family, whose chief seat is Lulworth Castle in Dorsetshire.[1] He was sent by his father in 1844

---

[1] "James Weld, Esq., seventh son of Thomas Weld, Esq.,

to S. Edmund's college, near Ware in Hertfordshire, for his education. He was a boy of great piety and virtue, and gave not only satisfaction to the masters of studies, but edification to all his fellow-students. It happened that on April 16, 1846, a play-day or whole holiday, the President of the college gave the boys leave to boat upon the river at Ware.

"In the morning of that day Philip Weld had been to the Holy Communion at the early celebration of Mass, having just finished his retreat. In the afternoon of the same day he went with his companions and some of the masters to boat on the river as arranged. This sport he enjoyed very much. When one of the masters remarked that it was time to return to the college, Philip asked whether they might not have one more row. The master consented, and they rowed to the accustomed turning-point. On arriving there, and in turning the boat, Philip accidentally fell out into a very deep part of the river; and, notwithstanding that every effort was made to save him, was drowned.

"His dead body was brought back to the college,

---

of Lulworth Castle, was born April 30, 1783, married July 15, 1812, the Hon. Juliana Anne, daughter of Robert Edward, tenth Lord Petre, and has had issue, 1. Henry, 2. Francis, a priest, 3. *Philip*, died 1846 ; 1. Anna Maria, 2. Katharine, 3. Agnes, a nun, 4. Charlotte."—See Burke's "Landed Gentry," vol. ii. art. "Weld of Lulworth Castle."

and the Very Rev. Dr. Cox, the President, was immensely shocked and grieved. He was very fond of Philip; but what was most dreadful to him was to have to break this sad news to the boy's parents. He scarcely knew what to do, whether to write by post, or to send a messenger. At last he determined to go himself to Mr. Weld at Southampton. So he set off the same evening, and, passing through London, reached Southampton the next day, and drove from thence to Archer's Lodge, Mr. Weld's residence.

"On arriving there and being shown into his private study, Dr. Cox found Mr. Weld in tears. The latter, rising from his seat and taking the doctor by the hand, said, 'My dear sir, you need not tell me what you are come for. I know it already. Philip is dead. Yesterday I was walking with my daughter Katharine on the turnpike road, in broad daylight, and Philip appeared to us both. He was standing on the causeway with another young man in a black robe by his side. My daughter was the first to perceive him. She said to me, "Look there, papa: there is Philip." I looked and saw him. I said to my daughter, "It is Philip, indeed; but he has the look of an angel." Not suspecting that he was dead, though greatly wondering that he was there, I went towards him with my daughter to embrace him; but a few yards being between us, while I was going up to him a labouring man, who was walking on the same causeway, passed between the apparition and the hedge, and as he went on I saw him pass through their apparent bodies, as if they were transparent. On perceiving this I at once felt sure that they were spirits, and going forward with my daughter to touch them, Philip sweetly smiled on us, and then both he and his companion vanished away.'"

"The reader may imagine how deeply affected Dr. Cox was on hearing this remarkable statement. He of course corroborated it by relating to the afflicted father the circumstances attendant on his son's death, which had taken place at the very hour in which he appeared to his father and sister. They all concluded that he had died in the grace of God, and that he was in happiness, because of the placid smile on his face.[1]

"Dr. Cox asked Mr. Weld who the young man was in the black robe who had accompanied his son, and who appeared to have a most beautiful and angelic countenance, but he said that he had not the slightest idea.

"A few weeks afterwards, however, Mr. Weld was on a visit to the neighbourhood of Stonyhurst in Lancashire. After hearing Mass one morning in

---

[1] The Right Rev. Monsignor Patterson, the present President of S. Edmund's college (A.D. 1872), kindly informs me that there is a memorial brass in front of the sanctuary of the chapel of that society, on which is figured a floriated cross, rising out of waves, with a label appended to it,—" Lord save me."

the chapel, he, while waiting for his carriage, was shown into the guest-room, where, walking up to the fireplace, he saw a picture above the chimney-piece, which, as it pleased God, represented a young man in a black robe with the very face, form, and attitude of the companion of Philip as he saw him in the vision, and beneath the picture was inscribed 'S. Stanislaus Kostka,'[1] one of the greatest saints of the Jesuit order, and the one whom Philip had chosen for his patron saint at his Confirmation. His father, overpowered with emotion, fell on his knees, shedding many tears, and thanking God for this fresh proof of his son's blessedness. For in what better company could he be than in that of his patron saint, leading him, as it were, into the presence of his Creator and his Saviour, from the dangers and temptations of this state of exile to

---

[1] S. Stanislaus Kostka was born on Oct. 28, 1550, his parents being John and Margaret Kostka, Polish nobles of wealth and repute. Miraculous signs foreshadowed his birth; and the holiness and purity of his early years betokened in a marked manner the favour of God towards this child. In his fourteenth year he went to Vienna to finish his studies at the Jesuit college. Here, his saintliness was so manifested forth by his conduct, that the Fathers said, "We have in our seminary an angel under the form of Stanislaus." Many miraculous favours are said to have been bestowed upon him by the hands of saints and angels, too numerous and lengthy to be recorded. He commenced his noviciate in the Jesuit college at Rome; where, after a short but edifying sojourn, he joyfully departed this life, aged 18 years, on the morning of August 15, 1568.

a condition of endless blessedness and happiness?"[1]

This is, perhaps, one of the most remarkable and best-authenticated recent cases of Spectral Appearances which has ever been narrated. The various independent testimonies dove-tailing together so perfectly, centre in the leading supernatural fact—the actual apparition in the daytime of a person just departed this life by sudden death, seen not by one only, but by two people, simultaneously; and seen in company with the spirit of a very holy and renowned saint, the chosen patron of the youth who had just been drowned. A more clear and conclusive example of the Supernatural it would be impossible to obtain.

The following case in certain particulars is not

---

[1] Mr. de Lisle, of Garendon Park, Leicestershire, in communicating to me the above narrative, writes as follows:—" I send you my account of the apparition of Philip Weld, according to my promise. I received it back this morning (July 17, 1872) from the Benedictine Convent at Athenstone, in Warwickshire, where my daughter Gwendoline is a nun, and where one of the Miss Welds, a cousin of Philip, is also a nun. She approves the accuracy of my account, and has added a paper with a few notes, which I inclose along with my own article, and from which you can correct mine so far as needed. I add here my affirmation that the above recorded narrative is a true and faithful account of what the Very Rev. Dr. Cox, then President of S. Edmund's College, related to me and to Mrs. de Lisle in February, 1847." The Editor is also greatly indebted to the Very Rev. Alfred Weld, S.J., for his courteous Letters upon the subject of the above narrative, as likewise to the Rev. E. J. Purbrick, S.J.

unlike that just recorded; for two persons, at a distance of many hundred miles apart, saw the Apparition of their departed relative who had just died in Australia :—

"Circumstances, in the year 1848," writes a correspondent of the Editor, "induced me to allow my youngest daughter to leave England, in order to join a son of mine in Australia, who had left home about five years previously, to seek his fortune in that country. In England, at home, he had every opportunity of making his way in life, and settling advantageously, but had availed himself of none that had offered. After leaving school, he was placed under a private tutor's care, and duly entered at Oxford. There he did nothing, or next to nothing, and left without taking any degree. Soon after this, at his own suggestion, in company with a friend, whose acquaintance he had made at the university, an acquaintance which eventually ripened into a warm friendship, he went to Australia; and he did not go empty-handed. A sum of money was placed to his credit with a colonial bank in the city of London having agencies in that colony, and nothing was left undone to secure for him a good start in his self-chosen and new life. I ought to add here that my own wish always had been that he should remain at home, and, after receiving orders, become vicar of a parish, the patronage of which was in the gift of a relation. Man proposes, but God disposes.

"In Australia, as was not otherwise than I myself had anticipated, the manner of life was utterly unlike that to which he had been accustomed. Ill-luck and want of success met him at every turn, as we afterwards found out; and not only did want of success meet him, but he had to undergo privations and hardships, which eventually weakened a constitution never too strong.

"At the time that I consented to my daughter going out, much of the above was unknown to us. He had written complaining of ill-health and weakness, and she, with great self-denial and sisterly devotion, resolved to go. She went with the understanding that she was soon to return. Just before she started, the mail brought us unexceptionally bad news of her brother's weak state of health, written by his college friend.

"About six weeks after her departure, I was sitting musing in my arm-chair, on a summer afternoon, close to the window of my library, which looked out upon a lawn, to the left of which were three large and overspreading cedar-trees. All of a sudden I saw the life-like apparition of my son standing below the cedar-trees. He looked very pale, thin, and careworn, much altered, but my very son. He gazed at me intently, and with a mournful gaze, for about the space of two minutes. I could not speak—I could not move—I could not take my eyes off him. I seemed riveted to the spot; and, of course, I was at once convinced of the fact that he had died. Then he seemed gradually to fade away. It was weeks before I could get the thoughts of his appearance out of my mind; and nothing that the members of my family could say served to remove the impression so indelibly stamped upon it of our loss.

"Some months afterwards, we received letters from my daughter (just landed) and his other friends in Australia announcing his decease. He had died somewhat suddenly, having expressed the most anxious desire to see me before his death—a desire repeated again and again, and regarding which he seemed to be unquiet.

"The most remarkable feature yet to be told in the circumstance was this,—that my daughter, who was reposing in the ladies' cabin of the ship, on her way to Australia, saw the apparition of her brother come into the cabin, move round it by a strange motion, and then, after looking at herself with a strained and mournful look, glide out again.

"Events afterwards showed that these appearances, both on shipboard and at my own home, occurred at or about the very time of my dear boy's death. And nothing will convince me that the record here set down is not one of the most remarkable and undoubted examples of supernatural apparitions. May God Almighty join us all together again, after these earthly separations, in His heavenly kingdom!"

The following example, which has already appeared in print, is authenticated by a personal acquaintance of the Editor, who has kindly written him a Letter on the subject. It was first given to Dr. William Gregory,[1] who published it about twenty-three years ago. It is said to have occurred in 1849:[2]—

"An officer occupied the same room with another officer in the West Indies. One night he awoke his companion, and asked him if he saw anything in the room, when the latter answered that he saw an old man in the corner whom he did not know. 'That,' said the other, 'is my father, and I am sure he is dead.' In due time news arrived of his death in England at that very time. Long afterwards the officer took his friend who had seen the vision to visit the widow, when, on entering the room, he started, and said, '*That is the portrait of the old man I saw.*' It was, in fact, the portrait of the

---

[1] "Letters on Animal Magnetism," by Dr. W. Gregory, pp. 448-489. London, 1851.

[2] "The Apparition or Spectral Appearance of my friend's father to him in the West Indies—the old gentleman having died in England, and the fact of two officers having seen it simultaneously, shows that it could not have been the result of their imagination, but that it was an objective appearance; in fact, the dead man's immortal spirit, indicating to one once bound by Nature's ties to the living witness of it, that the separation of soul and body had taken place. It is firmly believed by the family, who, however, all shrink from making their names public. So, my dear doctor, you must be content with this."—E. M. C., Cambridge, July 15, 1873.

father, whom the friend had never seen except in the vision."

"This story," writes Dr. Gregory, "I have on the best authority; and everyone knows that such stories are not uncommon. It is very easy, but not satisfactory, to laugh at them as incredible ghost stories; but there is a natural truth in them, whatever they may be."

Examples of Apparitions at the time of Death to friends and relations are, however, so numerous that a considerable number might readily be printed. Here are two, well and duly authenticated.

The following statement is vouched for by the person signing the same :—

"In the summer of 1816, my father and mother having retired to bed about nine o'clock, the latter was about to draw down the blind, when she observed the figure of a female approaching their house by a footpath which communicated with the village. Thinking the circumstance unusual, she waited till the figure approached sufficiently near to discern its features, when she exclaimed to my father, 'Why, here is my sister B——; what can have induced her to come here at this time of the evening?' She was about to prepare to go downstairs to inquire the cause of such a visit at that late time of night, when my mother observed the figure retracing its steps in the same direction by which it had come. The following morning, early, intelligence was brought to my mother that her sister B—— died at the same hour at which her apparition appeared to my mother. This is a simple statement of facts.

"Signed by the son of the person to whom the apparition appeared.

"C. J. Hanmer.
" 33, Henley Street, Camp Hill, Birmingham."

The following is another statement of facts vouched for by those who formally testify to its truth :—

"One evening in the autumn of the year 1868, my wife retired to bed early. On my entering the bedroom about midnight, I found her wide awake, and in a very excited state. On inquiring the cause, she stated that she believed most firmly she had seen our old friend Mrs. G——, then residing at a distance, whom we believed to be in perfect health. My wife gave a minute description of her dress, which I had remembered to have seen her wear, and at the same time stated that when the apparition appeared to her, every object in the bedroom was strangely but distinctly visible. Of course I tried to allay my wife's excitement by assuring her that she was suffering from the effects of an unpleasant dream, but I failed to shake her conviction that she had seen the spirit of our friend.

"Nothing occurred during the next day, but on the following we received a letter from a relative, stating that Mrs. G—— had died the night before about twelve o'clock.

"It appears that Mrs. G——, while in her garden, was observed to fall upon one of the flower beds. Having been taken to her room, medical aid was promptly procured, but without avail: she remained unconscious from that time until the moment of her death, which occurred about twelve o'clock the same evening.

"(Signed) C. L. Hanmer,
Catherine Hanmer
(Wife of the above).

"Branch Dispensary, Camp Hill, Birmingham,
Oct. 18, 1872."

The following Account of the Apparition of a murdered man, near the place of his death, is very remarkable. It has been published, though in another form, in Australia, and is there generally accepted as true. The version given below is from those who are thoroughly competent to furnish a true and faithful account of a very impressive narrative:—

"In Australia, about twenty-five years ago, two graziers, who had emigrated from England, and entered into partnership, became, as was generally believed, possessed of considerable property, by an unlooked-for success in their precarious but not unprofitable occupation. One of them all of a sudden was missed, and could nowhere be found. Search was made for him in every quarter, likely and unlikely, yet no tidings of him or his whereabouts could be heard.

"One evening, about three weeks afterwards, his partner and companion was returning to his hut along a bye-path which skirted a deep and broad sheet of water. The shadows of twilight were deepening, and the setting sun was almost shut out by the tall shrubs, brushwood, and rank grass which grew so thick and wild. In a moment he saw the crouching figure of his companion, apparently as real and life-like as could be, sitting on the ground by the very margin of the deep pond, with his left arm bent, resting on his left knee. He was about to rush forward and speak, when the figure seemed to grow less distinct, and the ashen-coloured face wore an unusually sad and melancholy aspect; so he paused. On this the figure, becoming again more palpable, raised its right arm, and, holding down the index finger of the right hand, pointed to a dark and deep hole, where the water was still and black, immediately beside an overhanging tree. This action was deliberately done, and then twice repeated, after which the figure, growing more and more indistinct, seemed to fade away.

"The grazier was mortally terrified and alarmed. For a while he stood riveted to the spot, fearing either to go forward or backward; while the silence of evening and the strange solitude, now for the first time in his Australian life thoroughly experienced, overawed him completely. Afterwards he turned and went home. Night, which came on soon, brought him no sleep. He was restless, agitated, and disquieted.

"The next morning, in company with others, the pool was dragged, and the body of his partner discovered, in the very spot towards which the figure of the phantom had twice pointed. It had been weighted and weighed down by a large stone attached to the body; while from the same spot was recovered a kind of axe or hatchet, with which the murder had evidently been committed. This was identified as having belonged to a certain adventurer, who, on being taxed and formally charged with the murder, and found to be possessed of certain valuable documents belonging to the murdered man, eventually confessed his crime, and was executed.

"This incident, and its supernatural occurrences, made a deep impression; and, having been abundantly testified to, in a court of justice, as well as in common and general conversation, is not likely to be soon forgotten in the neighbourhood of Ballarat, in Australia, where it occurred."

Here, of course, the purpose of the Apparition was obvious enough; and the end attained was as just and proper as it was true and righteous; for "whoso sheddeth man's blood, by man shall his blood be shed."

The following example of the appearance of the spirit of a dying woman to her children, who were at a distance of some hundreds of miles from her, is a plain unvarnished narrative of facts. It is now published for the first time.

"A lady and her husband (who held a position of some distinction in India) were returning home (A.D. 1854) after an absence of four years, to join a family of young children, when the former was seized in Egypt with an illness of a most alarming character; and, though carefully tended by an English physician and nursed with the greatest care, grew so weak that little or no hope of her recovery existed. With that true kindness which is sometimes withheld by those about a dying bed, she was properly and plainly informed of her dangerous state, and bidden to prepare for the worst. Of a devout, pious, and reverential mind, she is reported to have made a careful preparation for her latter end, though no clergyman was at hand to minister the last sacrament, or to afford spiritual consolation. The only point which seemed to disturb her mind, after the delirium of fever had passed away, was a deep-seated desire to see her absent children once again, which she frequently expressed to those who attended upon her. Day after day, for more than a week, she gave utterance to her longings and prayers, remarking that she would die happily if only this one wish could be gratified.

"On the morning of the day of her departure hence,

she fell into a long and heavy sleep, from which her attendants found it difficult to arouse her. During the whole period of it she lay perfectly tranquil. Sōon after noon, however, she suddenly awoke, exclaiming, 'I have seen them all: I have seen them. God be praised for Jesus Christ's sake!' and then slept again. Towards evening, in perfect peace and with many devout exclamations, she calmly yielded up her spirit to God Who gave it. Her body was brought to England, and interred in the family burying-place.

"The most remarkable part of this incident remains to be told. The children of the dying lady were being educated at Torquay under the supervision of a friend of the family. At the very time that their mother thus slept, they were confined to the house where they lived, by a severe storm of thunder and lightning. Two apartments on one floor, perfectly distinct, were then occupied by them as play and recreation rooms. All were there gathered together. No one of the children was absent. They were amusing themselves with games of chance, books, and toys, in company of a nursemaid who had never seen their parents. All of a sudden their mother, as she usually appeared, entered the larger room of the two, pausing, looked for some moments at each and smiled, passed into the next room, and then vanished away. Three of the elder children recognized her at once, but were greatly disturbed and impressed at her appearance, silence, and manner. The younger and the nursemaid each and all saw a lady in white come into the smaller room, and then slowly glide by and fade away."

The date of this occurrence, September 10, 1854, was carefully noted, and it was afterwards found that the two events above recorded happened almost contemporaneously. A record of the event was committed to paper, and transcribed on a fly-leaf of the family Bible, from which the above account was taken and given to the Editor of this book in the autumn of the year 1871, by a relation of the lady in question, who is well acquainted with the fact of her spectral appearance at Torquay, and has vouched for the truth of it in the most distinct and formal manner. The husband, who was reported to have been of a somewhat sceptical habit of mind, was deeply impressed by the occurrence. And though it is seldom referred to now, it is known to have had a very deep and lasting religious effect on more than one person who was permitted directly to witness it.[1]

A personal acquaintance of the Editor, whom he

---

[1] "The narrative of the spectral appearance of a lady at Torquay, forwarded to Dr. F. G. Lee at his special request, is copied from, and compared with that in, the family Bible of H. A. T. Baillie-Hamilton by the undersigned,

"C. Margaret Balfour,
Mary Baillie-Hamilton.
Witness, J. R. Grant.

"Princes Street, Edinburgh,
October 7, 1871."

has had the pleasure of knowing for twenty years, most kindly furnishes the following example:—

"In the winter of 1872-3 I was afflicted with a long and severe illness, so severe indeed, that for six weeks I was hovering between life and death. A nurse of great knowledge and intelligence was in attendance on me; she had been brought up as a Socinian, and was entirely careless as to religious belief. At the same time she was wholly devoted to her duties, and most attentive and assiduous in the same. Two days after her arrival she was sitting up in the adjoining room, the folding-doors between which and the room where I was lying being open, and lights were burning in each apartment. It had struck two o'clock a.m., and from my critical position she was unwilling either to sleep or to secure temporary rest. On looking up at that moment she perceived a form bending over me. The figure was that of an aged person with attenuated features, straggling grey hair, and thin clasped hands, which were placed in the attitude of prayer. For a while she thought it was someone who had entered the room; but, after gazing at it intently, she was smitten with a strange awe, and stood watching it attentively for at least five minutes, when it gradually faded away and disappeared.

"On the first opportunity she mentioned this strange occurrence to the people of the house, when she heard for the first time that my father had been lying dangerously ill at his own residence, more than a hundred miles away. At the time of my own and my father's sickness, my dangerous state, for medical and prudential reasons, was not communicated to him, and my illness was made light of, fearing the bad effect upon himself. That it was his Spirit which then appeared seems undoubted: for at two o'clock p.m. a relation came to see me from the City where my father had lived, to break to me the sad news of his decease. He had departed this life exactly at the period when his apparition in the attitude of prayer had been seen by my attendant. These facts were not made known to me until some time afterwards."[1]

The following story, no less interesting and impressive, appears in "The Life and Times of Lord Brougham, written by Himself," published a few years ago by Messrs. Blackwood and Co.:—

"'A most remarkable thing happened to me—so remarkable that I must tell the story from the beginning. After I left the High School [in Edinburgh], I went with G——, my most intimate friend, to attend the classes in the University. There was no divinity class, but we frequently in our walks discussed and speculated upon many grave sub-

---

[1] "The above is a correct and truthful statement.
"Witness my hand and seal.
John Gill Godwin.
"76, Warwick Street,
South Belgravia, Nov. 6, 1874."

jects—among others, on the immortality of the soul, and on a future state. This question and the possibility, I will not say of ghosts walking, but of the dead appearing to the living, were subjects of much speculation; and we actually committed the folly of drawing up an agreement, written with our blood, to the effect that whichever of us died first should appear to the other, and thus solve any doubts we had entertained of the "life after death." After we had finished our classes at the College, G—— went to India, having got an appointment there in the Civil Service. He seldom wrote to me, and after the lapse of a few years I had almost forgotten him; moreover, his family having little connection with Edinburgh, I seldom saw or heard anything of them, or of him through them, so that all the old schoolboy intimacy had died out and I had nearly forgotten his existence. I had taken, as I have said, a warm bath; and while in it and enjoying the comfort of the heat after the late freezing I had undergone, I turned my head round towards the chair on which I had deposited my clothes, as I was about to get out of the bath. On the chair sat G——, looking calmly at me. How I got out of the bath I know not, but on recovering my senses I found myself sprawling on the floor. The apparition, or whatever it was that had taken the likeness of G——, had disappeared. The vision produced such a shock that I had no inclination to talk about it, or to speak about it even to Stuart;

but the impression it made upon me was too vivid to be easily forgotten; and so strongly was I affected by it, that I have here written down the whole history with the date, 19th December, and all the particulars as they are now fresh before me. No doubt I had fallen asleep; and that the appearance presented so distinctly to my eyes was a dream, I cannot for a moment doubt, yet for years I had had no communication with G——, nor had there been anything to recall him to my recollection; nothing had taken place during our Swedish travels either connected with G—— or with India, or with anything relating to him or to any member of his family. I recollected quickly enough our old discussion, and the bargain we had made. I could not discharge from my mind the impression that G—— must have died, and that his appearance to me was to be received by me as a proof of a future state.' This was on December 19, 1799. In October, 1862, Lord Brougham added as a postscript:—'I have just been copying out from my journal the account of this strange dream: certissima mortis imago! And now to finish the story, begun about sixty years since. Soon after my return to Edinburgh there arrived a letter from India announcing G——'s death! and stating that he had died on the 19th of December.'"

The following example of the apparition of a departed friend is, for reasons which will be apparent from the narrative, not unlike the three curious, but independent cases already recorded in the early part of the present chapter, and not altogether unlike that told by the late Lord Brougham. It comes directly to the Editor from the pen of the person who saw the spectral appearance :—

"I was sitting in my library one evening, towards the close of summer, somewhat late. The shadow of evening had been deepening for some time, for the sun had long gone down; and the expansive valley beyond and below my sloping garden was white with mist. Within, beyond the heavy folds of the curtains which hung beside a single and rather small and open window, there was a grey darkness which almost enshrouded the corners of the room on either side. I had been musing and meditating on a variety of subjects, theological, metaphysical, and moral, for more than an hour; while I reposed in a low arm-chair on one side of the fire-place.

"All of a sudden I saw what seemed to be an elongated perpendicular cloud of foggy-looking grey smoke, collected in the right-hand corner of the room. I could not comprehend what it was. While looking steadily at it, and rubbing my eyes (doubting for a moment whether I was awake or asleep), it seemed to form itself, by a kind of circular rolling motion of the smoke or luminous mist, into a human shape. There, before me, came out slowly, as it were, face, head, body, arms, hands and feet—at first a little indistinct in detail, but eventually so self-evident and clear that it was impossible to doubt the fact—of a figure, which a moment or two afterwards was developed into the exact and unmistakeable form of an old fellow-student at Oxford, who had died soon after we left that university, and of whom I had heard nothing whatever since the day of his death about seven years previously,[1] to that moment. Appearing just as he had lived, though death-like and ashen, he looked at me with a fixed and strangely-vacant stare, which appeared to grow alternately vivid and piercing, and dull and nebulous. I seemed to feel the air all at once chill and unearthly; and an indescribable sensation came over me which I had never experienced either before or afterwards. I felt almost paralyzed, and yet not altogether terrified. The form of my old college companion (who had been a very upright, devout and religious man) in a moment smiled at me, and raising his hand, pointed for a few seconds upwards. At this action a very bright mist, not exactly a light, but a luminous mist, seemed to hover over him. I tried to speak, but could not. My tongue clave to the roof of my mouth. Then, protecting myself with the sign of the Cross, and a mental invocation of the Blessed Trinity, I sheltered my eyes

---

[1] Special enquiry, made since the above was penned, shows conclusively that this appearance was seen exactly seven years after the date of death.—Editor.

with my right hand for a few seconds, and then looking up again saw the apparition become more and more indistinct and soon altogether fade away.

"This is my ghost story, and I have always connected the appearance with arguments and conversations which, against aggressive objectors, used to be held at Oxford in defence of the Christian doctrines of the Resurrection of the Body and the Immortality of the Soul, in which my dead friend took so intelligent and earnest a part."

Not less interesting is the following account of a Spectral Appearance which occurred in the latter part of the afternoon of a bright autumnal day, well authenticated, and here set forth for the first time:—

"The widow of a well-known Bristol merchant was, in 1856, acting as lady housekeeper to a Berkshire clergyman. One of her sons was an officer in the Indian army, and serving in the Madras Presidency. It was his custom to write to his mother by every fortnightly mail. He had not missed doing so with punctual regularity.

"One evening, however, between six and seven, in the month of October of the above year, the lady in question was walking on the lawn before the house, in company with the curate of the parish, a well-known Oxford man, when all of a sudden both of them saw what appeared to be a dog-cart containing three men drive along the lane which skirted the lawn and flower-garden, and which was separated from it by a closely-cut box-hedge, so low as to admit of those who were walking in the garden seeing with ease and distinctness any person approaching the house in a vehicle. It was driven in the direction of the carriage entrance, and, from the sound, appeared to have entered the court-yard of the house. One of the persons in it, he who sat behind, half rose, and looking towards his mother and the clergyman, smiled, and waved his right hand as a greeting. He looked very pale and ashy; otherwise there was nothing remarkable in his appearance. Both most distinctly observed the action just mentioned. Immediately on seeing it, the lady exclaimed with marked feeling and excitement, 'Good heavens! why, there's Robert.' She at once rushed through a passage of the house, which led directly to the court-yard, only to find to her amazement and perplexity that no carriage nor dog-cart had arrived, and that the large gates of the house were, as usual, locked and fastened, and moreover had not been opened.

"The impression this remarkable incident made was deep and great. No doubt whatever existed in the minds of those who had seen and heard the passing vehicle, that the form on the seat behind was the son of the lady in question. She consequently felt confident that some harm had happened to him, became miserable, and was inconsolable. No remarks or reasoning to the contrary, several of which were attempted, produced the slightest effect. A deep gloom settled over her. The sequel can soon be narrated. In the course of a few weeks the mail *viâ* Southampton, most anxiously looked for, brought two letters to the lady in question, one intimating that her son had been suddenly struck with a most severe fever, was delirious and in great danger; the other intimating his death. This latter occurred on the very day at which the appearance in question was seen, but at a slightly different time."

With the following example, as strange in itself as it is painfully interesting, this part of the subject will be brought to a close. It is only right to add that a version of the incident which now follows has already appeared in one of Mr. Henry Spicer's interesting volumes:—

"A young German lady of rank, still alive to tell the story, arriving with her friends at one of the most noted hotels in Paris, an apartment of unusual magnificence on the first floor was apportioned to her use. After retiring to rest, she lay awake a long while contemplating, by the dim light of a night lamp, the costly ornaments in the room, when suddenly the folding doors opposite the bed, which she had locked, were thrown open, and amid a flood of unearthly light there entered a young man in the dress of the French navy, having his hair dressed in the peculiar mode *à la Titus*. Taking a chair, and placing it in the middle of the room, he sat down, and took from his pocket a pistol of an uncommon make, which he deliberately put to his forehead, fired, and fell back dead. At the moment of the explosion, the room became dark and still, and a low voice said softly, 'Say an *Ave Maria* for his soul.'

"The young lady fell back, not insensible, but paralyzed with horror, and remained in a kind of cataleptic trance, fully conscious, but unable to move or speak, until at nine o'clock, no answer having been given to repeated calls of her maid, the doors were forced open. At the same moment, the powers of speech returned, and the poor young lady shrieked out to her attendants that a man had shot himself in the night, and was lying dead on the floor. Nothing, however, was to be seen, and they concluded that she was suffering from the effects of a dream.

"A short time afterwards, however, the proprietor of the hotel informed a gentleman of the party that the terrible scene witnessed by the young lady had in reality been enacted only three nights previously in that very room, when a young French officer put an end to his life with a pistol of a peculiar description, which, together with the body, was then lying at the Morgue, awaiting identification. The gentleman examined them both, and found them exactly correspond with the description of the man and the pistol seen in the apparition. The Archbishop of Paris, Monseigneur Sibour, being exceedingly impressed by the story, called upon the young lady; and, directing her attention to the words spoken by the mysterious voice, urged her to embrace the Roman Catholic faith, to whose teaching, as His Grace asserted, it pointed so clearly.

The various examples of Spectral Appearances now given (and they might have been largely augmented) may certainly serve to provide cases, so inherently striking and conclusive in themselves, as to leave little or no doubt of their intrinsic truth. Making every allowance for unintentional misconceptions and exaggeration in the record of them, putting aside mere rhetorical ornaments and literary additions, it seems quite impossible, being guided by the ordinary rules of evidence, not to admit the force and value of such striking facts as the above. In the cases already set forth, it is quite irrational to maintain that the disturbed imagination or wild fancy of the persons who are said to have seen the Apparitions were the sole foundations of the things seen; more especially as in some instances the Appearances were beheld by two or more persons at the same time, and often the same form presented itself to different people upon different occasions. It may be that some own a power of seeing disembodied spirits, which is not possessed by others, and it is tolerably certain that the large majority of people have never beheld anything of the sort. But this, after all, is but negative testimony. That which is positive, covering, it may be, a small area, is of considerable value and importance in aiding those who are open to conviction in coming to a reasonable conclusion. For existing positive evidence cannot be rudely and arrogantly set aside, when found to be, as in the case under consideration, so completely in harmony with many of the plain and specific statements of Holy Scripture, with the express testimony of the Fathers of the Christian Church, and the almost universal tradition of mankind in every age.

HAUNTED HOUSES AND LOCALITIES.

"Nations civilized as well as uncivilized: barbarians of the rudest type, and Christians of the highest and deepest spirituality, have always believed that certain localities were the haunts of unquiet spirits."—Richard H. Froude.

CHAPTER VII.

HAUNTED HOUSES AND LOCALITIES.

MANY who are unaffected by the demoralizing and degrading materialistic theories of life, which are now enunciated by some who name themselves, and whom their flattering admirers style "philosophers," will not be unwilling to allow that a considerable amount of evidence[1] is in existence, indicating that certain localities are troubled by the presence of evil spirits, who from time to time manifest their powers, or sometimes appear to mankind in forms which give a shock to those who are enabled or permitted to perceive them.

---

[1] The Editor is in no degree concerned with Paganism or Pagan superstitions, nor has he gathered præ-Christian examples. Yet such will have been numerous to the ordinary student of classical history. The Haunted House of Damon, mentioned by Plutarch, will be familiar to many.

If Christian tradition be accepted, a belief in the official ministry of unfallen spirits,—"the armies of the Living God,"—will be held, firmly[1] and intelligibly, as a most reasonable and beautiful part of Almighty God's revelation, Who "has ordained and constituted the services of angels and men in a wonderful order." So, by consequence, the existence and action of fallen angels, the Legions of Satan, and of spirits,[2] who, at the particular judg-

---

[1] The following is the original of a most beautiful verse in Bishop Ken's well-known "Evening Hymn," either mutilated in the worst of taste in most hymn-books, or else altogether eliminated and suppressed :—

> "You, my best guardian, while I sleep
> Close to my bed your vigils keep ;
> Your love angelical instil,
> Stop all the avenues of ill."

[2] "What do we know of the World of Spirits? Little or nothing, beyond what Faith and Revelation afford. Still we know that they surround us ; that they hover over us ; that they accompany us whithersoever we go ; and that even in the innermost tabernacle of the soul they penetrate and have their being. Good spirits and bad are around us ; good spirits to aid us, to waft our lame and imperfect prayers to heaven, and to protect us in the hour of temptation or peril. 'He shall give His angels charge over thee, lest thou dash thy foot against a stone.' Bad angels, too, are around us and against us, percolating through every avenue of the soul, inflaming the imagination, warping the judgment, tainting the will, and too often, alas ! perverting it to perdition. Bad angels are around us, even within the protecting sanctuary of God's Church, when summoned, permitted there by the subdued and corrupted will of man. Bad angels are around us in every walk and rank and condition and event of life : we see

ment following immediately upon death, have merited the swift and righteous condemnation of an all-just Judge, will be fully admitted.

The power, activity, and malice of Satan is apparent from numerous statements in Holy Scripture; and most Christian writers who have dealt with the subject of evil spirits have maintained that their power and influence are unquestionably greater in some localities than others. It is commonly held, that in lonely deserts, on lofty mountains, where the feet of men seldom tread, as well as in the mines of the earth,[1] and in vast forests where desolation reigns, the powers of the Devil and his angels, being unchecked and uncurbed by the positive energizing activity of Christianity, are vast. So, likewise, the universal instinct of mankind has maintained that

---

them not, but they hover over us and around us, and they penetrate within the mysterious precincts of the soul, by many a foul and unholy thought, by many an evil suggestion to sin. And they triumph, and they gibber in their unholy glee whenever they tempt and prevail. They triumph, and they laugh the insulting laugh whenever they steep to the lips in sin an unhappy mortal, and fasten upon him the mocking thought and determination of a deathbed repentance. That is their battle ground, the battle ground of victory. The standard of deceit is then triumphant: the captive is delivered bound into their hands to do with as they list, to be tormented according to the refinement of their infernal pleasure. 'He shall be delivered unto the tormentors.'"—Rev. Edward Price.

[1] This belief prevails extensively in Sweden, Germany, and Switzerland.

there are certain places in which the appearances of unquiet or lost souls might be reasonably looked for, rather than in others. Deserted houses and lonely roads, where crimes of violence and special wickedness have been perpetrated; deep mines,[1] localities, unblessed by Holy Church, where the bodies of Christians have been placed to moulder away, instead of in God's holy acre, the consecrated churchyard; battlefields, where it may be that so many have been cut off in deadly sin—

"Unhouseled, disappointed, unanealed,"

have each and all been regarded as the fitting haunts of disquieted and wandering spirits.

On this point Southey, in "The Doctor," with much force thus writes:—"The popular belief that *places* are haunted where money has been concealed (as if, where the treasure was and the heart had been, there would the miserable soul be also), or where some great and undiscovered crime has been committed, shows how consistent this is with our natural sense of fitness."

---

[1] The souls of the dead, or spirits of some sort, are constantly heard and not unfrequently seen in mines. A Shropshire miner informed the Editor that, of his own knowledge, he had heard supernatural sounds of moanings and mutterings underground, and had seemed to *feel* the passing spirits as they swept by. On one occasion, after the violent and sudden death of a comrade, the noises were unusually loud; while the horses employed underground would stand trembling and covered with perspiration whenever the spirits were heard.

On a collateral detail of this subject (the constant and malignant activity of evil spirits), Mr. John Wesley, a thorough believer in the Supernatural, put forth his faith and convictions with singular force and lucidity, plainly maintaining the reality and importance of all those explicit statements of Holy Scripture which so directly and practically bear on the point under treatment.

"Let us consider," wrote Wesley, "what may be the employment of unholy spirits from death to the resurrection. We cannot doubt but the moment they leave the body, they find themselves surrounded by spirits of their own kind, probably human as well as diabolical. What power God may permit these to exercise over them we do not distinctly know. But it is not improbable [that] He may suffer Satan to employ them as he does his own angels, in inflicting death or evils of various kinds on the men that know not God. For this end they may raise storms by sea or by land; they may shoot meteors through the air; they may occasion earthquakes; and in numberless ways afflict those whom they are not suffered to destroy. Where they are not permitted to take away life, they may inflict various diseases; and many of these, which we may judge to be natural, are undoubtedly diabolical. I believe this is frequently the case with lunatics. It is observable that many of these, mentioned in the Scripture, who are called 'lunatics' by one of the Evangelists, are termed 'demoniacs' by another. One of the most eminent physicians I ever knew, particularly in cases of insanity, the late Dr. Deacon, was clearly of opinion that this was the case with many, if not with most lunatics. And it is no valid objection to this, that these diseases are so often cured by natural means; for a wound inflicted by an evil spirit might be cured as any other, unless that spirit were permitted to repeat the blow. May not some of these evil spirits be likewise employed, in conjunction with evil angels, in tempting wicked men to sin, and in procuring occasions for them? Yea, and in tempting good men to sin, even after they have escaped the corruption that is in the World. Herein, doubtless, they put forth all their strength, and greatly glory if they conquer."[1]

Although some may maintain that this passage is perhaps wanting in theological exactness, there can be little doubt that, with much force, it truly and eloquently embodies the belief of all Christian people, and gives a simple and forcible explanation of Scripture statements regarding the active and untiring energy of the legions of Hell.

Again, the Marquis de Marsay, a pious French Protestant writer of the last century, whose collected works were issued about the year 1735, sets forth from his own point of view a theory regard-

---

[1] "The Life of the Rev. John Wesley, M.A., by Robert Southey, Esq.," vol. ii. p. 370. London: 1858.

ing the nature and character of spirits, which because it bears directly on the subject of Haunted Localities, and in some respects follows the teaching of the schoolmen, it may be well to quote here:—

"I believe," he writes, "that there are three kind of spirits, which return to this World, after the death of their bodies. The spirits of such as are in a state of condemnation, and which are in a very miserable condition, hover about, and *haunt the places where they have committed their evil deeds and iniquities.* They remain at these places by divine permission, and do all the evil they can; whilst, at the same time, they suffer intolerable torments and are malignant. Some of this kind of spirits occasionally make themselves visible. . . . . The second kind of spirits are those which roam about, because they seek to free themselves from their state of purification[1] by other means than by

---

[1] In many places on the continent, especially in France and Spain, it was the custom to pray for departed souls, suffering (as their needful purification was incompleted) *in any particular locality*. Dr. Neale gives an example of this, occurring in a prayer which he saw printed and hung up in a church at Braganza in Spain, which ran thus:—"We pray, likewise, for the souls which are suffering in any place by the particular chastisement of God." And the following is translated from a French Prayer-Book of the last century:—"Have mercy, O Lord God, good and pitiful, on the souls of those who are being chastised for their transgressions in the flesh, in those places where Thou willest them

resignation to Divine Justice; hence they seek help from those that fear God, and in so doing, withdraw themselves from the Divine Order. . . . . These are not evil spirits, but such as are still in their self-will, and therefore refuse to yield to the Divine Order, by voluntarily submitting themselves to the punishment imposed upon them. . . . *The third kind of spirits, or rather souls that reappear, are those, whose punishment is to be at some certain place in this world, because they have satisfied their passions in that place, and lived according to their lusts in an idolatrous manner;* for that which now causes a man lust and pleasure, must hereafter serve as his pain and punishment. Of this we have several instances; amongst others, that of a pious man, who after his death appeared to his daughter, who was likewise a pious person, and after conversing with her some time on his state, began to turn pale, to tremble, and be much distressed; and said to his daughter that the time was now arrived when he must go and remain for a time in his grave, with his putrefying and corrupting corpse; and that this happened to him every day, because in his life-time he had had too much affection and tenderness for his body."

The dissertations of the schoolmen, and of certain English writers of the seventeenth century,

---

to suffer;" an evident reference in both cases to troubled spirits which haunt definite spots.

are not unlike the above.[1] So, too, are several of their most reasonable deductions and conclusions. In fact, Dr. Joseph Hall, sometime Bishop of Exeter (A.D. 1627-1641, and afterwards of Norwich, from 1641 until 1656), maintained that many souls, guilty both of deadly sin (duly repented of during life), and of venial sin, in which not improbably they died, might have to suffer, by lingering, unsatisfied, because away from their Creator,

---

[1] When the tone of thought in Shakspeare's day is compared with that in our own, the contrast between the accurate and explicit religious statements regarding the Supernatural, with the shallow and cynical scepticism of modern writers, can hardly be put down to the credit of the Modern. At all events those who claim to range themselves on the side of the Ancient and the True may be permitted to do so. Nothing could more forcibly set forth the current belief of the sixteenth century than the following well-known utterance of the Ghost in " Hamlet " :—

" I am thy Father's spirit ;
Doom'd for a certain time to walk the night,
And for the day confined to fast in fires,
Till the foul crimes done in my days of nature
Are burnt and purged away. But that I am forbid
To tell the secrets of my prison-house,
I could a tale unfold whose lightest word
Would harrow up thy soul, freeze thy young blood,
Make thy two eyes, like stars, start from their spheres,
Thy knotted and combined locks to part,
And each particular hair to stand on end,
Like quills upon the fretful porcupine :
But this eternal blazon must not be
To ears of flesh and blood."
     " Hamlet," pp. 22-23. Oxford : 1873.

and about the places where they sinned in their lifetime, until their temporal punishment was complete; a theory which though from the pen of one suspected of favouring Puritanism, is very like that embodied in the faith and practice of the Universal Church.

However this may be, at all events there is scarcely a locality in which some old tradition as regards Haunted Houses and Places does not exist; and which is not more or less accepted and believed in even now. A general rejection of the Supernatural may be the case with many, and a shallow desire not to be thought superstitious or over-credulous by more, are obvious reasons why some traditions have become weakened and others obscure. But putting aside all such, half-lost, forgotten, or fading away, and making every allowance for exaggeration and hyperbole, the facts which can still be testified to by credible witnesses, the evidence which is even now on record, coupled with that innate sentiment of awe, so common to many, and often strengthened by a sound religious belief, which gives point to old traditions, are sufficient to induce the calm and the unprejudiced not too hastily to disavow the existence of a principle of almost universal acceptance with mankind, and which neither the lame and limping logic of the sceptic, nor the imperfectly marshalled facts and random conclusions of the materialist can, in the long run, either weaken or destroy.

The following curious record, a fair example of numerous others, may now be suitably set forth:—

"Elizabeth, the third daughter of Sir Anthony Cooke (preceptor to Edward VI.) married Sir Thomas Hobby, of Bisham Abbey in Berkshire, and accompanied him to France, when as ambassador to Queen Elizabeth he went thither. On his death abroad in 1566 Lady Hobby brought his corpse home to Bisham, where he was buried in a mortuary chapel. She afterwards married John, Lord Russell. By her first husband she had a son, who when quite young is said to have entertained the greatest dislike and antipathy to every kind of learning; and such was his resolute repugnance to acquiring the art of writing that in a fit of obstinacy he would wilfully and deliberately blot his writing-books in the most slovenly manner. Such conduct so vexed and angered his mother, who was eminently intellectual, and like her three sisters, Lady Burleigh, Lady Bacon, and Lady Killigrew, an excellent classical scholar, that she beat him again and again on the shoulders and head, and at last so severely and unmercifully that he died.

"It is commonly reported that, as a punishment for her unnatural cruelty, her spirit is doomed to haunt the house where this cruel act of manslaughter was perpetrated. Several persons have seen the apparition, the likeness of which, both as regards feature and dress, to a pale portrait of her ladyship in antique widow's weeds still remaining at Bisham, is said to be exact and lifelike. She is reported to glide through a certain chamber, in the act of washing blood stains from her hands. And on some occasions the apparition is said to have been seen in the grounds of the old mansion.

"A very remarkable occurrence in connection with this narrative, took place about thirty years ago. In taking down an old oak window-shutter of the latter part of the sixteenth century, *a packet of antique copy-books of that period were discovered pushed into the wall between the joists of the skirting, and several of these books on which young Hobby's name was written, were covered with blots, thus supporting the ordinary tradition.*"[1]

Creslow in Buckinghamshire,[2] like so many old manor-houses, has its ghost story. It is said to be the disturbed and restless spirit of a lady, which haunts a certain sleeping chamber in the oldest portion of the house. She has been seldom seen but often heard only too plainly by those who have ventured to sleep in this room, or to enter it

---

[1] The Editor is indebted to the late Revs. W. Hastings Kelke and H. Roundell of Buckingham, for the above curious example. It was intended to have been published some years ago in "The Records of Bucks."

[2] For an accurate account by the late Rev. W. Hastings Kelke of this curious and interesting old mansion, the property of Lord Clifford of Chudleigh, see "The Records of Bucks," vol. i. pp. 255-267. Aylesbury, 1858.

after midnight. She appears to come up from the old groined crypt, and always enters by the door at the top of the nearest staircase. After entering she is heard to walk about, sometimes in a gentle, stately manner, apparently with a long silk train sweeping the floor. Sometimes her motion is quick and hurried, her silk dress rustling violently as if she were engaged in a desperate struggle.

This chamber, though furnished as a bedroom, is seldom used, and is said to be never entered without trepidation and awe. Occasionally, however, some persons have been found bold enough to dare the harmless noises of the mysterious intruder; and many are the stories current in Buckinghamshire respecting such adventures. The following will suffice as a specimen, and may be depended on as authentic :—

"About the year 1850, a gentleman, not many years ago High Sheriff of the county, who resides some few miles' distance from Creslow, rode over to a dinner-party; and, as the night became exceedingly dark and rainy, he was urged to stay over the night if he had no objection to sleep in the haunted chamber. The offer of a bed in such a room, so far from deterring him, induced him at once to accept the invitation. He was a strong-minded man of a powerful frame and undaunted courage, and like so many others, entertained a sovereign contempt for all haunted chambers, ghosts, and apparitions. The room was prepared for him. He would neither have a fire nor a night-light, but was provided with a box of lucifers that he might light a candle if he wished. Arming himself in jest with a cutlass and a brace of pistols, he took a serio-comic farewell of the family and entered his formidable dormitory.

"In due course, morning dawned; the sun rose, and a most beautiful day succeeded a very wet and dismal night. The family and their guests assembled in the breakfast-room, and every countenance seemed cheered and brightened by the loveliness of the morning. They drew round the table, when the host remarked that Mr. S—, the tenant of the haunted chamber, was absent. A servant was sent to summon him to breakfast, but he soon returned, saying he had knocked loudly at his door, but received no answer, and that a jug of hot water left there was still standing unused. On hearing this, two or three gentlemen ran up to the room, and, after knocking and receiving no answer, opened it and entered. It was empty. Inquiry was made of the servants; they had neither seen nor heard anything of him. As he was a county magistrate, some supposed that he had gone to attend the Board which met that morning at an early hour. But his horse was still in the stable; so that could not be While they were at breakfast, however, he came in, and gave the following account of his last night's experiences:—'Having entered my room,' said he, 'I locked and bolted both the doors, carefully examined the whole room, and satisfied myself that there was no living creature in it but myself, nor any entrance but those which I had secured. I got into bed, and, with the conviction that I should sleep soundly as usual till six in the morning, was soon lost in a comfortable slumber. Suddenly I was awakened, and, on raising my head to listen, I certainly heard a sound resembling the light soft tread of a lady's footstep, accompanied with the rustling as of a silk gown. I sprang out of bed, and having lighted a candle, found that there was nothing either to be seen or heard. I carefully examined the whole room. I looked under the bed, into the fire-place, up the chimney, and at both the doors, which were fastened just as I had left them. I then looked at my watch, and found it was a few minutes past twelve. As all was now perfectly quiet again, I put out the candle, got into bed, and soon fell asleep. I was again aroused. The noise was now louder than before. It appeared like the violent rustling of a stiff silk dress. A second time I sprang out of bed, darted to the spot where the noise was, and tried to grasp the intruder in my arms. My arms met together, but enclosed nothing. The noise passed to another part of the room, and I followed it, groping near the floor to prevent anything passing under my arms. It was in vain, I could feel nothing. The sound died at the doorway to the crypt, and all again was still. I now left the candle burning, though I never sleep comfortably with a light in my room, and went to bed again, but certainly felt not a little perplexed at being unable to detect the cause of the noise, nor to account for its cessation when the candle was lighted."

So that this gentleman's experience (and as to ghosts, he was a sceptic) only served to strengthen the old and unbroken tradition. Of its foundation nothing very certain is known. The general facts, however, are commonly received.

Another example, unusually curious, relating to the Castle at York, is taken from the "Memoirs of Sir John Reresby:"—

"One of my soldiers being on guard about eleven in the night at the gate of Clifford Tower, the very night after the witch was arraigned, he heard a great noise at the Castle; and, going to the porch, he saw there a scroll of paper creep from under the door, which, as he imagined by moonshine, turned first into the shape of a monkey, and thence assumed the form of a turkey-cock, which passed to and fro by him. Surprised at this, he went to the prison, and called the under-keeper, who came and saw the scroll dance up and down, and creep under the door, where there was scarce an opening of the thickness of half-a-crown. This extraordinary story I had from the mouth both of one and the other."[1]

---

[1] " Memoirs of Sir John Reresby," p. 238.

An account of the haunting of Spedlin's Tower was furnished to me by a Scotch friend, who asserts and vouches for the authenticity of the tradition :—

"Spedlin's Tower, the scene of one of the best accredited and most curious ghost stories perhaps ever printed, stands on the south-west bank of the Annan, in Dumfriesshire. The ghost story is simply this :—Sir Alexander Jardine, of Applegarth, in the time of Charles II., had confined in the dungeon of his tower of Spedlin's, a miller named Porteous, suspected of having wilfully set fire to his own premises. Sir Alexander being soon after suddenly called away to Edinburgh, carried the key of the vault with him, and did not recollect or consider his prisoner's case till he was passing through the West Port, where, perhaps, the sight of the warder's keys brought the matter to his mind. He immediately sent back a courier to liberate the man, but Porteous had, in the meantime, died of hunger.

"No sooner was he dead, than his ghost began to torment the household, and no rest was to be had within Spedlin's Tower by day or by night. In this dilemma, Sir Alexander, according to old use and wont, summoned a whole legion of ministers to his aid; and by their strenuous efforts, Porteous was at length confined to the scene of his mortal agonies, where, however, he continued to scream occasionally at night, 'Let me out, let me out, for I'm deein' o' hunger!' He also used to flutter against the door of the vault, and was always sure to remove the bark from any twig that was sportively thrust through the key-hole. The spell which thus compelled the spirit to remain in bondage was attached to a large black-lettered Bible, used by the exorcists, and afterwards deposited in a stone niche, which still remains in the wall of the staircase; and it is certain that, after the lapse of many years, when the family repaired to a newer mansion (Jardine Hall), built on the other side of the river, the Bible was left behind, to keep the restless spirit in order. On one occasion, indeed, the volume requiring to be rebound, was sent to Edinburgh; but the ghost, getting out of the dungeon, and crossing the river, made such a disturbance in the new house, hauling the baronet and his lady out of bed, &c., that the Bible was recalled before it reached Edinburgh, and placed in its former situation. The good woman who told Grose this story in 1788, declared that should the Bible again be taken off the premises, no consideration whatever should induce her to remain there a single night. But the charm seems to be now broken, or the ghost must have become either quiet or disregarded, for the Bible is at present kept at Jardine Hall."

'Another example from Scotland now follows, all the more remarkable, because it is still asserted that in a certain part of the mansion unusual voices, and supernatural footsteps are said to be still heard, a fact to which the late Mr. Hope Scott often testified:—Sir Walter Scott relates a striking occurrence which happened to him at the time Abbotsford was in the course of erection. Mr. Bullock was then employed by him to fit the castle up with proper appurtenances, when during that person's absence in London the following extraordinary circumstance took place:—In a letter to Mr. Terry in the year 1818 Scott wrote:—" The night before last we were awakened by a violent noise like drawing heavy boards along the new part of the House. I fancied something had fallen and thought no more about it. This was about two in the morning. Last night at the same witching hour the same noise recurred. Mrs. S., as you know, is rather timbersome; so up I got with Beardy's broadsword under my arm,

'Sat bolt upright
And ready to fight.'

But nothing was out of order; neither could I discover what occasioned the disturbance." Now, strangely enough on the morning that Mr. Terry received this letter he was breakfasting with Mr. Erskine (afterwards Lord Kinneder) and the chief subject of their conversation was the sudden death of Mr. Bullock, which on comparing dates must have happened on the same night and as near as could possibly be ascertained at the same hour, these disturbances occurred at Abbotsford. One might be induced to maintain that some drunken workmen or disorderly persons were on the premises, but this method for accounting for the coincidence will at once be exploded on reading the following passage from Scott to the same gentleman:—" Were you not struck with the fantastical coincidence of our nocturnal disturbance at Abbotsford with the melancholy event that followed? I protest to you that the noise resembled half-a-dozen men hard at work pulling up boards and furniture, *and nothing could be more certain than that there was nobody on the premises at the time.*"

The following account of a haunted locality is from the pen of a scholarly and accomplished clergyman[1] in the diocese of Ripon:—" Some years ago I was residing in a village about eleven miles from York, and one mile and a half from another village, in which was the Post Office for the surrounding district. Whenever I had reason to suppose a letter was lying there for me, I used to anticipate the delivery of it on the following morning, by calling for it myself in the evening before. One night, in the latter end of November, I was going, for this purpose, along the path through the fields, and when I was midway between the two villages, I passed through a little hand-gate, and after going about twenty yards from it, I was startled and

---

[1] The Rev. Joseph Jefferson, M.A., Vicar of North Stainley, near Ripon, who sent me the above—unaltered, and printed just as it was written—on the 2nd of June, 1873.

alarmed by a succession of the most horrible shrieks that can possibly be conceived. They seemed scarcely human, though I felt at the time that they were certainly uttered by some man or woman, imitating the piercing scream of a hog when the fatal knife is being plunged into its throat. The panic that seized me vanished in a moment, as the thought instantaneously flashed across my mind that I was being made the victim of some plough-man's joke. Being armed, as I then invariably was, with a particularly tough and stout cudgel, I ran back to the little hand-gate on tip-toe, intending to take condign vengeance on some rustic, whom I felt sure I should find crouching down behind the low hedge. Just as I reached the hand-gate, the sounds suddenly ceased, and to my utmost astonishment I could see no one, although it was quite impossible for any person within the distance of two or three hundred yards to have escaped my observation. The full moon was shining brightly, with the very thinnest of fleecy clouds before her face, which did not obscure her light, but only made the whole country distinctly visible in every direction, from the absence of all strongly-defined shadow. Then, again, I must confess, an unaccountably superstitious awe crept over me, and, instead of pursuing my intended route, I returned to my own home.

"On the following morning, when reflecting on what had happened, I began to take a philosophical and reasonable view of the singular occurrence. In passing through the little gate I might, as I thought, have left it ajar, and that soon after it lost its nice equilibrium, and swung back to its accustomed resting-place. The hinges might have given a creaking sound, which the lonely solitude of the night had intensely magnified in my imagination. So much for the philosophical view. I then determined that I would put this view to the proof, and see if I could by any means get the gate to produce any noise similar to what I fancied I had heard. This was the reasonable view. I took care, however, to put my determination into practice at the earliest period of the evening, just, in fact, as the daylight had departed. Accordingly I was at the little gate between five and six o'clock, but in spite of all kinds of efforts it would make no sign, but swung backwards and forwards on its hinges with noiseless smoothness. In the midst of my experiments a very intelligent man, a Gardener by calling, came up. He was a resident of my own village, but had been working in the other village, and was then returning home from his day's labour. He expressed some surprise at seeing me there at that time of the evening, and I gave him a brief account of the reason. 'Well, sir,' said he; 'if you will walk back with me, I will tell you something more about that little hand-gate.' I consented immediately, and he said to me as follows: 'Some years ago, when we were all children at home, my mother had been to the other village, where she remained till night; on her return homewards, just as she passed through the little gate, she saw some kind of figure lying close by it, huddled together in a strange, mysterious manner. She was horror-stricken, and fled from the spot as fast as possible. On reaching her own cottage, she flung open the door, and fell fainting on the ground before her astonished and frightened children. When she came to herself, and was asked what had caused her evident terror, she told what she had seen, and where she had seen it. She could, however, give no definite description of the figure she had seen. She could only say, " It was something hideous." But never could she be induced to pass that place again after night-fall, as long as she lived.' 'Well,' said I, 'this is a very remarkable coincidence.' 'Yes,' said he, 'but I will tell you something more remarkable still. About forty years ago the land between the two villages was unenclosed. It was nothing more than a wild, uncultivated common. One night, about that period, as the villagers were going to bed, loud and piercing shrieks were heard coming from the common. Some of the men dressed themselves hastily, with the intention of going and seeing what was taking place. Some woman, as it seemed to them, was evidently being ill-treated. They set off on their kindly-intentioned errand, but as the sounds completely ceased, and the night was very dark, they thought it impossible to reach the exact spot where their services might be required. They went to bed, and slept soundly. On the following morning one of them was going to work at the other village, and as he passed over the common he was almost distilled to a jelly with the effect of fright at the appalling sight that suddenly met his gaze. A woman was lying before him, huddled up on the ground, quite dead, with her throat cut from ear to ear. She had evidently been murdered, on the preceding night. Who she was, whence she came, why or by whom she had been murdered, was never known, and probably never will be in this world. When, a short time after this dreadful event, the common was enclosed, it so happened that the little hand-gate was put up close to the spot where the woman's lifeless body was found.'

"He finished his narrative. I thanked him for it, and internally resolved never, if I could help it, to pass through those fields alone in the gloom of night, on any account whatever. I scrupulously kept my resolve."

The celebrated case of the Haunted Room in the Jewel House of the Tower of London created great interest, about fifty-five years ago. Additional interest and importance have been given to it by the publication of the following authentic account of Mr. E. Lenthal Swifte,[1] which in simple but forcible language tells its own story:—

---

[1] "Notes and Queries," vol. x. second series, Sept. 8, 1860, pp. 192-193, and Sept. 22, 1860, p. 236.

"I have often purposed to leave behind me a faithful record of all that I know personally of this strange story. . . . . . Forty-three years have passed, and its impression is as vividly before me as on the moment of its occurrence. . . . . . In 1814 I was appointed keeper of the Crown Jewels in the Tower, where I resided with my family until my retirement in 1852. One Saturday night in October, 1817, about 'the witching hour,' I was at supper with my then wife, our little boy, and her sister, in the sitting room of the Jewel House, which—then comparatively modernized—is said to have been 'the doleful prison' of Anne Boleyn, and of the ten bishops whom Oliver Cromwell piously accommodated therein. . . . . . The room was, as it still is, irregularly shaped, having three doors and two windows, which last are cut nearly nine feet deep into the outer wall; between these is a chimney-piece projecting far into the room, and (then) surmounted with a large oil picture. On the night in question the doors were all closed; heavy and dark cloth curtains were let down over the windows, and the only light in the room was that of two candles on the table. . . . . . I sate at the foot of the table, my son on my right hand, his mother fronting the chimney-piece, and her sister on the opposite side. I had offered a glass of wine and water to my wife, when, on putting it to her lips, she paused and exclaimed, 'Good God, what is that?' I looked up, and saw a cylindrical figure like a glass tube, seemingly about the thickness of my arm, and hovering between the ceiling and the table. Its contents appeared to be a dense fluid, white and pale azure, like to the gathering of a summer cloud, and incessantly rolling and mingling within the cylinder. This lasted about two minutes, when it began slowly to move *before* my sister-in-law, then following the oblong shape of the table, before my son and myself; passing *behind* my wife it paused for a moment over her right shoulder (observe, there was no mirror opposite to her in which she could then behold it). Instantly she crouched down, and, with both hands covering her shoulder, she shrieked out, 'Oh, Christ! it has seized me.' Even now, while writing, I feel the fresh horror of that moment. I caught up my chair, struck at the wainscot behind her, rushed upstairs to the other children's room, and told the terrified nurse what I had seen. . . . . Neither my sister-in-law nor my son beheld this 'appearance.' . . . I am bound to add that shortly before this strange event some young lady residents in the Tower had been, I know not wherefore, suspected of making phantasmagorical experiments at their windows, which, be it observed, had no command whatever on any windows in my dwelling. An additional sentry was accordingly posted so as to overlook any such attempt. Happening, however, as it might, following hard at heel the visitation of my household, one of the night sentries at the Jewel Office was, as he said, alarmed by a figure like a huge bear issuing from underneath the door. He thrust at it with his bayonet, which stuck in the door, even as my chair dinted the wainscot. He dropped in a fit, and was carried senseless to the guard-room. His fellow-sentry declared that the man was neither asleep nor drunk, he himself having seen him the moment before awake and sober. Of all this I avouch nothing more than that I saw the poor man in the guard-house prostrated with terror, and that in two or three days the fatal result, be it of fact or fancy, was that he died. Let it be understood that to *all* which I have herein set forth *as seen by myself*, I absolutely pledge my faith and my honour.—Edmund Lenthal Swifte."

Another statement, regarding another apparition in the same part of the Tower, stated by Mr. Offor to have been produced by some instrument, but which latter assertion is pronounced impossible by Mr. Lenthal Swifte, also sufficiently illustrates the facts embodied in it :—

"Before the burning of the armouries there was a paved yard in front of the Jewel House, from which a gloomy and ghost-like doorway led down a flight of steps to the Mint. Some strange noises were heard in this gloomy corner ; and on a dark night at twelve the sentry saw a figure like a bear cross the pavement and disappear down the steps. This so terrified him that he fell, and in a few hours after, having recovered sufficiently to tell the tale, he died. It was fully believed to have arisen from phantasmagoria. . . . . . . The soldier bore a high character for bravery and good conduct. I was then in my thirtieth year, and was present when his body was buried with military honours in the Flemish burial ground, St. Catherine's.

" George Offor."

On this, however, Mr. Swifte thus writes:—

"When on the morrow I saw the unfortunate soldier in the main guard-room, his fellow sentinel was also there, and testified to having seen him on his post just before the alarm, awake and alert, and even spoken to him. Moreover, as I then heard the poor man tell his own story, the figure did not cross the pavement and disappear down the steps of the sally-port; but issued from underneath the Jewel Room door—as ghostly a door, indeed, as ever was opened to or closed on a doomed man; placed, too, beneath a stone archway as utterly out of the reach of my young friends' apparatus (if any such they had) as were my windows. I saw him once again on the following day, but changed beyond my recognition; in another day or two—*not* 'in a few hours'—the brave and steady soldier, who would have mounted a breach or led a forlorn hope with unshaken nerves, died at the presence of a shadow, as the weakest woman might have died.

" Edmund Lenthal Swifte."

The case of a Haunted House in Northamptonshire may now follow:—

"A house at Barby,[1] a small village about eight miles from Rugby, was reputed to be haunted, and this under the following circumstances:—An old woman of the name of Webb, a native of the place, and above the usual height, died on March 3, 1851, at two A.M. aged sixty-seven. Late in life she had married a man of some means, who having predeceased her, left her his property, so that she was in good circumstances. Her chief and notorious characteristic, however, was excessive penuriousness, being remarkably miserly in her habits; and it is believed by many in the village that she thus shortened her days. Two of her neighbours, women of the names of Griffin and Holding, nursed her during her last illness, and her nephew, Mr. Hart, a farmer in the village, supplied her temporal needs; in whose favour she had made a will, by which she bequeathed to him all her possessions.

"About a month after the funeral Mrs. Holding, who, with her uncle, lived next door to the house of the deceased (which had been entirely shut up since the funeral), was alarmed and astonished at hearing loud and heavy thumps against the partition wall, and especially against the door of a cupboard in the room wall, while other strange noises,

---

[1] Barby is a parish in the Hundred of Fawsley, in the county of Northampton, a little more than five miles from Daventry. It contains between six and seven hundred inhabitants.

like the dragging of furniture about the rooms (though all the furniture had been removed), and the house was empty. These were chiefly heard about two o'clock in the morning.

"Early in the month of April a family of the name of Accleton, much needing a residence, took the deceased woman's house, the only one in the village vacant, and bringing their goods and chattels, proceeded to inhabit it. The husband was often absent, but he and his wife occupied the room in which Mrs. Webb had died, while their daughter, a girl about ten years of age, slept in a small bed in the corner. Violent noises in the night were heard about two o'clock, thumps, tramps, and tremendous crashes, as if all the furniture had been collected together, and then violently banged on to the floor. One night at two A.M. the parents were suddenly awakened by the violent screams of the child, 'Mother, mother, there's a tall woman standing by my bed, a-shaking her head at me!' The parents could see nothing, so did their best to quiet and compose the child. At four o'clock they were again awakened by the child's screams, for she had seen the woman again; in fact she appeared to her no less than seven times, on seven subsequent nights.

"Mrs. Accleton, during her husband's absence, having engaged her mother to sleep with her one night, was suddenly aroused at the same hour of two by a strange and unusual light in her room. Looking up she saw quite plainly the spirit of Mrs.

Webb, which moved towards her with a gentle appealing manner, as though it would have said, 'Speak, speak!'

"This spectre appeared likewise to a Mrs. Radbourne, a Mrs. Griffiths, and a Mrs. Holding. They assert that luminous balls of light hovered about the room during the presence of the spirit, and that streams of light seemed to go up towards a trap-door in the ceiling, which led to the roof of the cottage. Each person who saw it testified likewise to hearing a low, unearthly, moaning noise,—'strange and unnatural-like,' but somewhat similar in character to the moans of the woman in her death-agony.

"The subject was, of course, discussed; and Mrs. Accleton suggested that its appearance might not impossibly be connected with the existence of money hoarded up in the roof, an idea which may have arisen from the miserly habits of the dead woman. This hint having been given to and taken by her nephew, Mr. Hart, the farmer, he proceeded to the house, and with Mrs. Accleton's personal help made a search. The loft above was totally dark, but by the aid of a candle there was discovered, firstly, a bundle of writings, old deeds, as they turned out to be, and afterwards a large bag of gold and bank-notes, out of which the nephew took a handful of sovereigns, and exhibited them to Mrs. Accleton. But the knockings, moanings, strange noises, and other disturbances did not cease upon this discovery. They did cease, however, when Mr. Hart, having found that certain debts were owing by her, carefully and scrupulously paid them. So much for the account of the Haunted House at Barby. The circumstances were most carefully investigated by Sir Charles Isham, Bart., and others, the upshot of which was that the above facts were, to the complete satisfaction of numerous enquirers, completely verified."

The following comes to the Editor from Scotland :—

"There is, without a doubt, a 'Haunted Room' in Glamis Castle. Access to it now is cut off by a stone wall, and none are supposed to know where it is, except Lord Strathmore, his eldest son, and the Factor on the estate. This wall was built some years ago by the present proprietor. Strange, weird, and unearthly noises have been heard from time to time by numbers, and these by many persons wholly unprepared for the same. The following statement is from the lips of a lady who was sleeping in the castle one night, and who knew nothing of the reputation of the house :—She was undressing to retire for the night, when all of a sudden she was alarmed by a most violent noise, which made her fancy that one of the walls of the house had fallen. She rushed out into the passage, but no one but herself had been aroused by it. So she went back, and slept until morning. She mentioned the circumstance at breakfast, but the subject was evidently an unpleasant one. The conversation was at once changed, and she received a hint to take no further notice of it. Some members of the family cannot bear the subject to be alluded to, and repel all inquiries."

"There is no doubt," writes another correspondent, "about the reality of the noises at Glamis Castle. On one occasion, some years ago, the head of the family with several companions was determined to investigate the cause one night, when the disturbance was greater and more violent and alarming than usual. His lordship went to the Haunted Room (before it was walled up), opened the door with the key, and dropped back in a dead swoon into the arms of his companions; nor could he be ever induced to open his lips on the subject afterwards.

"On another occasion a lady and her child were staying for a few days at the castle. The child was asleep in an adjoining dressing-room, and the lady, having gone to bed, lay awake for a while. Suddenly a cold blast stole into the room, extinguishing the night-light by her bedside, but not affecting the one in the dressing-room beyond, in which her child had its cot. By that light she saw a tall mailed figure pass into the dressing-room from that in which she was lying. Immediately thereafter there was a shriek from the child. Her maternal instinct was aroused. She rushed into the dressing-room, and found the child in an agony of fear. It described what it had seen as a giant, who came and leant over its face.

"An accomplished antiquarian, who has investigated this subject, writes as follows:—There is a tradition that in olden times, during one of the frequent feuds between the Lindsays and the Ogilvies, a large number of the latter, in flying from their enemies, came to Glamis, and claimed hospitality. The master of the castle did not like to deny them the protection of his castle walls. He therefore admitted them; and on plea of hiding them, is reported to have put them into this out-of-the-way chamber. There he let them starve, and it is said that their bones lie there unto this day, the bodies never having been buried. This may have been the sight which startled the late Lord Strathmore on entering the haunted room—a large number of skeletons lying in the various parts of the place was a sight calculated to startle any man. And these are declared to be peculiarly revolting. Some had apparently died in the act of gnawing the flesh off their own arms."

The Editor is indebted to Henry Cope Caulfeild, Esq., of Clone House, St. Leonard's, for the following:—

"The account here set forth was recently told to me by a Captain S—— living near Cardiff, South Wales.

"A few miles from Cardiff, on the Monmouth

road, there is a narrow spot held in awe by the peasantry; for a murder was committed there years ago, and it is said to be haunted by unquiet spirits.

"The brother of my friend, an officer in the army, who has seen active service in India, was returning with his wife in a dog-cart, some few months ago, from a dinner with some friends in the country a few miles from Cardiff. It was late in the night; and as they entered the narrow part of the road just mentioned, they heard the sound of wheels behind them. They looked back, and saw the lights of a carriage, and to avoid being overtaken and passed in such a narrow road, Captain S—— whipped his horse, and tried to keep well in front. Presently the sounds of wheels ceased; and to their great surprise, indeed consternation, they all of a sudden saw the lights and heard the wheels of a carriage some distance on in front of them. It was evidently the same; and yet it had never passed them! It seemed to stop at the side of the road, and Captain S—— drove his dog-cart past the strange carriage. He and his wife saw in it a dim light; there were people in it, and they seemed to be without heads! Mrs. S—— was paralysed with terror; her husband told his brother that he would rather face a battery of artillery than go through the horror of that moment; and the horse evidently was in sympathy with them, for he went like one mad.

"It appears that the very same spectral figures

had been seen by a country surgeon when passing the same place; and that the land-owners in those parts had cut down trees, and clipped and altered the appearance of the hedges on each side of the road, in order to get rid, if possible, of the ghastly horror, and of the hold which it has upon the popular mind. The *appearance* of the carriage and its occupants, in a dim, hazy light, was to the last degree unearthly and spectral."

A correspondent of the Editor furnishes him with the following:—

"A brother of mine, a man who is the last person in the world to believe over much, or to be in the least degree superstitious, wishing to be near a particular town, and yet within easy reach of the permanent country residence of his greatest friend, was induced (A.D. 1862) to take over the remainder of the lease of an old-fashioned furnished mansion in Cheshire, where he, with his wife, children, and servants, in due course, went to reside. He was advised to take the place as well because of the reasonableness of the rent—for it was spacious and comfortably furnished—as by the recommendation of the London house-agents, a well-known firm in the West End, with whom the letting of it rested.

"Soon after the arrival of the family and servants, the latter protested again and again that they were disturbed almost every night by a continual 'tramp, tramp, tramp' of heavy footsteps up the stairs, and along the narrow passage, out of which were the doors which led to their bedrooms. They would have it that the house was haunted. The sounds were sometimes so loud and alarming that, as one of the servants remarked, 'It seemed like a regiment of foot soldiers marching over creaking boards.' Complaints were made to my brother, who merely said that the noises must be the result of wind under the joists, or of rats, and he laughed at the whole affair. Some of the servants gave warning, and left. Still the sounds went on: not always, and every night, but, with certain cessations, from time to time.

"In the autumn of the year 1863, a lady, her daughter of fourteen, and a maid, came to stay in the House; and as the former was somewhat of an invalid, a suite of rooms in the west wing, each communicating with the other, was apportioned to them. The second night after their arrival, the lady in question, suddenly awaking, saw in her bedroom a luminous cloud, which gradually appeared to be formed into the shape of an old man, with a most painfully depressing countenance, full of the deepest sorrow, and wearing a large full-bottomed wig. She tried to raise herself in bed, to see if it were not the effect of her half-waking fancy, or the result of a disturbed dream, but could not. The room, in which there was no natural light, seemed to be partially but quite sufficiently illuminated; and she felt confident that a spectre was before her. She gazed at it for some minutes, three at least, hearing the ticking of her watch, and counting the seconds. There the apparition stood, and seemed to be making an effort to speak, while a strange, dull, inarticulate groan seemed to come up as from the floor. Upon this, seeing the bell-rope hanging within the folds of the curtains at her right hand, she braced herself up to seize it and give it a most violent pull. Immediately she did this, the face of the figure bore an expression of anger, and by degrees it faded away. The bell, which hung some distance away, was heard by no one, and she was compelled to lie alone, for she feared to rise (though the apparition did not reappear) until the church clock near struck four, when, the morning having broken, she rose, and dressed herself.

"In the morning, before she had said a word, her daughter, on meeting her, said, 'Oh, mamma, an old man in a great wig tramped through my room twice in the night. Who could it have been?'

"The lady being so impressed by these occurrences, which her host and hostess would persist in saying were only the result of her own fancy, determined on leaving in the course of a few days (as she afterwards stated). On the following night, she slept with a night-light, and the door into her maid's room open. But the noise of tramping, which had been hitherto heard only in the servants' wing of the house, which was opposite, was now heard in the east side of it. 'Tramp, tramp, tramp!' the sounds were heard constantly, without cessation; so much so that the master of the house, my brother, rose suddenly that very night, thinking that thieves had broken in, and rushed out to the east passage. But all in a moment, they stopped; nothing was to be heard, nothing seen; all was still. This occurred again and again.

"The lady left as arranged. The noises ceased for a while, and then began once more. It was with difficulty that any of the servants could be induced to remain, believing that the house was haunted.

"About ten months afterwards, my brother having forgotten all about the supposed spectre and the noises, had been out for the day, and returned home in a dog-cart, some time after midnight, in company with his groom. Only the housekeeper had remained out of bed, as his return was quite uncertain. The horse and trap were put up, both the servants had gone to their rooms, and my brother was taking some refreshment in the housekeeper's apartment, by the light of the fire, when all of a sudden, a loud and decisive rap was heard at the door. Thinking, of course, that it was one of the servants, he replied, 'Come in.' Before the words were out of his mouth, the door opened, and the apparition of the old man in a large wig stood before him. My brother was paralysed with terror for a while. He could not speak; he tried hard, as he says, but his mouth was dry and his tongue motionless. 'Good God!' he exclaimed at length, 'am I awake or asleep, in my senses or gone mad?' The motionless figure, whose face was intensely sad, looked at him beseechingly. 'In God's Name, what do you want, or what can I do for you?' 'Too late! nothing,' was the mournful, but somewhat inarticulate response. And with that the spectre suddenly vanished away. At this moment a strong, loud, piercing, bitter wail, as of the voice of a woman, broke the awful silence. It seemed to come from the courtyard outside, and was repeated again and again round the upper part of the house. The scream was said to be like nothing human. The servants heard it, my sister-in-law was awoke by it, and the groom and housekeeper, with the others, as a consequence, came rushing downstairs. My brother, who is as brave and bold as he is remarkable for common sense, does not now dispute the reality of haunted houses.

"A few months afterwards, he and his left. And after he had given up possession, he was informed, on good and credible authority, that tradition confidently asserted the mansion to have been the residence of a disreputable Dutch hanger-on of William of Orange, who is represented to have violently made away with one of his mistresses in that very house, in a room which overlooked the park, now a disused lumber-room, at the east end of the old mansion."[1]

An American clergyman, of what is commonly termed "the Protestant Episcopal Church," sent the following, which, as he writes, "went the round of the newspapers," and for the truth of which he himself vouches:—

"Few positions in life can be imagined more disagreeable than that of being imprisoned in a haunted cell in a police station. 'The New Orleans Times' tells a most unpleasant story of a ghost-infested cell in the Fourth Precinct police station in that city. It appears that several years ago 'a little old woman,' named Ann Murphy, committed suicide by hanging herself in this cell; and since that event no fewer than thirteen persons have attempted to destroy themselves in a similar manner; four of these attempts being attended with fatal results. One of those lately cut down before life was extinct was a girl named Mary Taylor,

---

[1] "Your account, as about to be printed, is *true and exact*, as to all the facts of the haunted house at ——, which came within my own personal knowledge. Don't mention names, or we shall perhaps be damaging the property, and lay ourselves open to an action at law. I may add that the late Bishop of Chester [Dr. Graham] is said to have furnished a mutual friend, the late Master of Trinity, with similar accounts, which had taken place before I knew the place, verifying to an A B C the old and, no doubt, perfectly true tradition. It is strange enough I know, *but it is true.*—Yours, &c., H. S. B., November, 1874."

who, on recovering consciousness, declared that while lying on the floor of the cell she was aroused by a little old white woman in a faded calico dress, with no stockings and down-trodden slippers, with a faded handkerchief tied round her head. Her faded dress was bound with a sort of reddish-brown tape, and her hand was long, faded, and wrinkled, while on the fourth finger of her left hand was a plain, thin gold ring. 'This little woman,' said the girl, 'beckoned me to get up, and impelled me by some mysterious power to tear my dress in strips, place one of the strips round my neck, and tie the other to the bars. I lifted my feet from the floor, and fell. I thought I was choking, a thousand lights seemed to flash before my eyes, and I forgot all until I found myself in the room with the doctors and police bending over me. It was not until then that I really comprehended what I had done, and was, I believe, under a kind of trance or influence at the time, over which I had no control.' Mary Taylor had never heard of the suicide of Ann Murphy, whose appearance, according to the police, tallied exactly with the description given by the girl. Others having complained in a like manner of the ghostly occupant of the cell, the police, to test the real facts of the case, placed a night lodger who had just arrived in the city in this cheerful apartment. Being thoroughly tired and worn out, he fell asleep immediately, but shortly afterwards rushed into the office in a state of terrible alarm.

He, too, had been visited by the little old woman, and wisely declined to sleep another hour in the station."

The following case, as may be seen from an attestation at its conclusion, is likewise well authenticated :—

"An English clergyman, who was seeking a residence in a northern Scottish city about ten years ago, had his attention accidentally called to an old-fashioned, pleasant-looking detached house, of some size and convenience, which had been for some time vacant, about a mile and a-half from the city. It had considerable grounds round it well timbered, a high-walled garden, and was in many respects both commodious and comfortable. One attraction, likewise, was the extremely moderate rent which was asked for it. So he secured a lease of it for a short term of years. He and his family and servants came up from England in due course, and took up their abode in it. They were not there long before it soon became evident, to some of them at least, that the house was haunted. Noises of the most extraordinary character were heard in various parts. Sometimes there came the sound of heavy footsteps on the stairs. At others there were knocks, both violent and gentle, at the doors, none of which could be accounted for. At midnight, on several occasions, there was a constant, uninterrupted sound in one room, as if a large sledge-hammer (having been wrapped in a blanket folded several times), was steadily and regularly struck against the wall, at the head of the bed in the room, by some particularly powerful arms. 'Thump, thump, thump,' it sounded, as though lifted and directed with tremendous force; and this noise often lasted, with only slight intermission, for two or three hours. On other occasions persons on the stairs or in the passages felt the air move, and heard the creaking of the floor close to them, as if someone invisible were passing quickly by. One night, between twelve and two, the master and mistress of the family were awakened by a loud and startling noise, as if all the shutters of the windows of the house had been suddenly and simultaneously burst open with the greatest violence. The crash was literally tremendous; and each believed that thieves were breaking in. So the clergyman, seizing a large presentation sword which hung on the wall of the landing, unsheathed it, and went downstairs with a light, expecting to face the intruders. He first examined the dining-room (from whence the noise seemed chiefly to come), but everything was just as usual. No shutter was open; no cupboards forced. So, too, in hall and library. Nothing was moved. Then he descended into the large cellars; but there, likewise, everything was untouched, and nothing unusual was seen. A large retriever dog, which lay at the foot of the front stairs, however, was greatly agitated, trembled and howled. But still nothing was to be seen. Perfect silence reigned. So the clergyman and his wife returned to their sleeping-room, only to hear, all of a sudden, precisely the same strange noise repeated about ten minutes after their return, with, if anything, even greater violence.

It was currently reported, and commonly believed by several residents thereabouts, that many years previously, the cast-off mistress of a Scotch nobleman, having been handed over to a physician and university professor for marriage, and the latter having received from the nobleman in consideration of the marriage the gift of the house and lands in question, subsequently murdered the woman, for whom he had conceived a special dislike, and buried her body on the premises. This story, with slight but unimportant variations, was told by several; and it is quite certain that a young female Scotch servant, who once lived in the house, following the sound of heavy footsteps up to an attic in the front portion of the house, which she had pledged herself to do when next she heard them, fell down in a swoon or fit at the top of the stairs; from that moment lost her reason, and is now in a lunatic asylum, near the City in question. These are facts testified to by those who know the circumstances.[1] As to the general accuracy of the

---

[1] The wife of the clergyman above alluded to, wrote to the Editor as follows :—" Having read the account which

foregoing, the Editor is enabled, on the testimony of several, to pledge his word thereto.

I am indebted for the following narrative to a friend,[1] who in her own words has given all the details of another remarkable example of a Haunted House :—

"Monsieur de Goùmoëns, a magistrate, or a gentleman holding a high judicial position at Berne in Switzerland, a man of undoubted and well-established character for personal courage, as well as for moral rectitude, related to my father, Mr. Caulfeild of Bath, with whom he was on the most intimate terms of personal friendship, the following circumstance, at once so extraordinary and so painful, which had come within the precincts of his own house, as to drive him from his place of residence. The account was given to my father in the year 1829, when he was residing with his family at Berne. Noises and disturbances had been frequently heard in M. de Goumoëns' bedroom, as of footsteps, the opening and shutting of drawers, and of an escritoire when papers were shuffled about. The heavy curtains of the large old four-posted bed were drawn and undrawn by no human

---

you contemplate publishing, I can testify of my own personal knowledge that it is *neither understated nor exaggerated, but is in all its details strictly true and accurate.*— June, 1874."

[1] Miss S. F. Caulfeild, author of "Avenele," "Desmond," &c.

hand, and were sometimes suddenly flung up on to the top of the bed; while the sound of the flapping of the wings of some very large bird was often heard. All these and other sounds so disturbed M. de Goumoëns and his wife, that the health of the latter began perceptibly and seriously to fail. Examinations of the house made by himself, in conjunction with the police, and special investigations of the bedroom and other adjoining apartments, afforded no solution whatsoever of the mystery. At length Madame de Goumoëns' maid gave warning to leave her service, complaining that her sleep and peace were completely broken by these supernatural occurrences. While consulting together as to what could be done, and hesitating as to whether they might not be compelled to leave the place, the strange sounds became louder than ever. One night they were suddenly aroused by hearing sharp cries of distress from one of their children, a little boy, who slept in their room, and who in great terror called out fretfully again and again, 'Let me alone; let me alone; don't you hurt me!' as he pointed into vacancy. This particular event was the last straw which broke the camel's back, and led the child's parents to determine on leaving the house immediately.

"I may add that on a subsequent and more searching examination of the house, one room was found to be both locked and fastened up; regarding the character of which the owner was somewhat reticent.

However, the boarding before the door, which had been papered over, was removed, the keys were forthcoming, and the room was carefully examined. On the shutters being opened, it was found just as it had been left since its occupation by a previous tenant, who had gone by the sobriquet of 'the Black Styger.' He was a nobleman of bad reputation, and had committed suicide in that very apartment by blowing out his brains; the traces of which with blood were found scattered both on wall and floor. It was generally believed that his disturbed spirit haunted the place."

One of the most singular recent examples, testified to by two independent eye-witnesses, now deserves to be reproduced. The appearance of a large spectral bird is thus recorded by Mr. Henry Spicer in one of his curious and thoughtfully written volumes entitled "Strange Things amongst Us:"—

"Captain Morgan, a gentleman of the highest honour and veracity, and who certainly was not over-gifted with ideality, arrived in London one evening in 18—, in company with a friend, and took up his lodgings in a large old-fashioned house of the last century, to which chance had directed them. Captain Morgan was shown into a large bed-chamber, with a huge four-posted bed, heavy hangings, and altogether that substantial appearance of good, solid respectability and comfort which associated itself with our ideas of the wealthy burghers and merchants of the time of Queen Anne and the first George, when so many strange crimes of romantic daring or of deep treachery stained the annals of the day, and the accursed thirst for gold, the bane of every age, appeared to exercise its most terrific influence.

"Captain Morgan retired to bed, and slept, but was very soon awaked by a great flapping of wings close beside him, and a cold, weird-like sensation such as he had never before experienced spread through his frame. He started, and sat upright in bed; when an extraordinary appearance declared itself in the shape of an immense black bird, with outstretched wings, and red eyes flashing as it were with fire.

"It was right before him and pecked furiously at his face and eyes so incessantly, that it seemed to him a wonder that he was enabled, with his arms and the pillow, to ward off the creature's determined assaults. During the battle it occurred to him that some large pet bird belonging to the family had effected its escape, and been accidentally shut up in the apartment.

"Again and again the creature made at him with a malignant ferocity perfectly indescribable; but though he invariably managed to baffle the attack, he noticed that he never once succeeded in *touching* his assailant. This strange combat having lasted several minutes, the gallant officer, little accustomed to stand so long simply on the defensive, grew irritated, and leaping out of bed, dashed at his enemy.

The bird retreated before him. The captain followed in close pursuit, driving his sable foe, fluttering and fighting, towards a sofa which stood in the corner of the room. The moonlight shone full into the chamber, and Morgan distinctly saw the creature settle down, as if in terror, upon the embroidered seat of the sofa.

"Feeling now certain of his prey he paused for a second or two, then flung himself suddenly upon the black object, from which he had never removed his gaze. To his utter amazement it seemed to fade and dissolve under his very fingers. He was clutching the air; and in vain he searched, with lighted lamp, every nook and corner of the apartment, unwilling to believe that his senses could be the victims of so gross a delusion—no bird was to be found. After a long scrutiny the baffled officer once more retired to rest, and met with no further disturbance.

"While dressing in the morning, he resolved to make no allusion to what he had seen, but to induce his friend, on some pretext, to change rooms with him. That unsuspecting individual readily complied, and the next day reported, with much disgust, that he had had to contend for possession of the chamber with the most extraordinary and perplexing object[1] he had ever encountered, to all appear-

---

[1] It seems that other places are reported to be haunted by appearances of Birds. A correspondent informs the Editor

ance a huge black bird, which constantly eluded his grasp, and ultimately disappeared, leaving no clue to its mode of exit."[1]

And with this, the present chapter is closed.

---

that this is the case with an old House in Dorsetshire, not far from Poole, where a wingless bird is sometimes seen. The same is said of a mansion in Essex, as another correspondent declares. In one room in an old house in Dean Street, Soho, likewise, several persons have seen a large raven, three times the size of an ordinary raven, perched on the tester of the old-fashioned bed. The inmates of the house, in 1854, whose family had had the lease for eighty years, are said to have been so accustomed to seeing it (though they knew it to be spectral) that they were undisturbed by its frequent appearance. Dr. Neale's story as follows (not unlike the examples already given), is very singular. Regarding it he wrote :—
"*It comes to me with a weight of evidence, which, strange as is the tale, I cannot disbelieve.* Three friends, not very much distinguished by piety, had been dining together at the residence of one of them in Norfolk. After dinner they went out and strolled through the churchyard. 'Well,' said a clergyman, one of the three, 'I wonder, after all, if there is any future state or not?' They agreed that whichever died first should appear to the others and inform them. 'In what shape shall it be?' asked one of the friends. At that moment a flight of crows arose from a neighbouring field. 'A crow is as good a shape as any other,' said the clergyman; 'if I should be the first to die, I will appear in that.' He *did* die first; and some time after his death, the other two had been dining together, and were walking in the garden afterwards. A crow settled on the head of one of them, stuck there pertinaciously, and could only be torn off by main force. And when this gentleman's carriage came to take him home; the crow perched on it, and accompanied him back."

[1] "Strange Things Amongst Us." By Henry Spicer. 2nd ed., pp. 100-102. London: Chapman & Hall, 1864.

Numerous other cases of Haunted Localities might have been provided; some which have long been in print, others which have been heard from the lips of those whose experience and good faith testify to the truth of their narratives. In so many examples collected, almost every one owns certain features in common: and all in some measure are alike. Repetition, by consequence, becomes wearisome. The cases here put on record, therefore, while sufficiently diversified, serve abundantly to set forth the reality of those facts, to a brief record of which this chapter has been devoted.

MODERN SPIRITUALISM.

"Now the Spirit speaketh expressly that, in the latter times, some shall depart from the Faith, giving heed to seducing spirits and doctrines of devils."—1 *Tim.* iv. 1.

"Many believe that the final assault upon Christianity will be made by the enemies of God, bonded and compacted together into an universal kingdom. It may be, as some have held, that another Incarnation shall take place; and that the Enemy of souls will be permitted to assume man's nature. Anyhow, we are told that Antichrist shall *reign*. Thousands, deluded by false miracles and lying wonders, will become his subjects, his willing votaries; and own him as their king. His worship will be an adroit counterfeit of the worship of the True God—his kingdom a parody of the Catholic Church; while its doctrines will be at once so attractive and delusive to fallen man as that the predicted Apostasy will be great and widespread."—*Sermons on Antichrist.*

CHAPTER VIII.

MODERN SPIRITUALISM.

WHEN, in a country where for at least twelve centuries the Christian Religion has been accepted, and by which that country has received unknown blessings both temporal and spiritual, schools of thought arise, in which Historical Christianity is not simply patronized, but put out of court, the phenomenon is both portentous and noteworthy. That this is so at the present time in England with many, need scarcely be pointed out. The scepticism which has deluged the Continent, coming upon a people whose religious convictions had been so seriously disturbed by the Reformation, and whose conceptions of objective political truth had been so ruthlessly disorganized by the events of the Commonwealth and the Revolution of 1688, has found the ground well prepared for a scattering of the seeds of doubt. Abroad they were sown some generations ago, and brought forth deadly fruit. The French Revolution and its horrors followed as a matter of course. Events before our eyes tell in very plain language that our own turn has at last come.[1] The day

---

[1] The following is taken from a small volume which has been gratuitously circulated very widely amongst the clergy and laity. It bears a Christian title, but is altogether anti-Christian from end to end :—

"The unwise, idolatrous, early Christian priests, in their admiration of Christ, exalted him in their imagination to be God Himself, forgetting the Creator God, and exalting in their foolish imagination his Blessed Mother as the Mother of God—folly that has been widely perpetuated down to these days. Oh, foolish churches, how great has been your folly, how widely you have departed from the truth ; therefore how little you have been able to cope with the wicked heart of man !

"In like manner as the Israelites, from the crucifixion down to these days, have erred in disbelieving the Messiah-ship of Christ, so the spurious churches have, during many ages, exalted Christ in their imagination to be God. The Israelites and the spurious churches being equal in their great error—the one refusing to acknowledge him as the long-promised Messiah, the other exalting him in their imagination as being the Messiah, the Holy Ghost, and God the Creator also ; the Israelites refusing to give any glory to Christ, the spurious churches madly rushing, in their ancient antagonism towards the Jews, to the opposite extreme, by robbing, in their imagination, God the Creator of His Glory, and giving all glory to the Messiah, to the great grief of the Messiah.

"Now clearly understand, oh ye nations of the whole world! it was not God who was born out of the Virgin Mary, and who was crucified, but the before holy angel Christ—understand this, and the Holy Scriptures will be plain to your comprehension—Christians have erred greatly during

of trial is now upon us. True, the vulgarity of the eighteenth-century unbelievers is not at present so manifestly apparent; though it exists amongst certain active leaders of the lower classes with whom scepticism is popular. But the tone and temper of public opinion, the bold utterances of serials and newspapers, the public political policy now in vogue and popular, the too general understanding that Christianity is to be as far as possible ignored in legislation—all indicate the steady and rapid progress of sceptical liberalism.

The Broad Church party in the established communion has done much, and will no doubt do much more, to eliminate the Supernatural from the minds of its admirers and of the people of England. Dis-

---

so many generations, in like manner as the followers of Mahomet and of Buddah have erred—errors that were carelessly accepted by powerful rulers, evil and ignorant, and forced upon the priests and the people, generation after generation. The time is at hand, even knocking at the door, when your understanding shall be made clear, and neither the professing followers of Christ, nor of Buddah, nor of Mahomet, nor the unwise of other sects, will continue in their many errors."—" Christ is Coming," pp. 135-6.

"Yet to-day, if one dare question the value of Christianity, what a howl is raised from one end of Christendom to the other! We say so advisedly, for it is the howl of fear.... Though Christianity to-day declines and is losing power and vigour, yet in its day it hath done great and glorious good in the work of human redemption. It was an advance upon the religions which preceded it."—"What of the Dead? An Address by Mr. J. J. Morse, in the Trance State," p. 5. London: J. Burns. 1873.

liking dogma, its teaching, when the fog which surrounds it allows that teaching to be partly comprehended, is of the earth earthy. It dovetails in with the low material views and carnal desires of the money-grubbing many. Its ideal of bliss, not always wrapped up in philosophical jargon (and therefore sometimes intelligible), is simply commercial prosperity and temporal wealth; eating and drinking, marrying and giving in marriage, comfort, material pleasure and ease; the conquest of Nature by scientific research and progress; an enjoyment of the present and only the present; and a complete banishment of the old-world theology—useful, it may have been, in times gone by, when the World was being educated; but now to be thrown aside as lumber, worn out and valueless. In place of that Historical Christianity accepted since the days of S. Augustine of Canterbury, we are promised doubt, disbelief, a refined as well as an unrefined intellectual Paganism; and in the end—though such an end may not now be contemplated by all members of that ecclesiastical school—a positive rejection of the distinct nature of God.

At present, of course, the figure is decently draped. Its ugly proportions and hateful outline are not apparent. Its admirers have to accommodate themselves with some skill to the strong prejudices of the age; to tolerate systems which they contemn, to carry out the silent but certain operation of destruction, under the hypocritical desire of assisting mankind to complete the work of temporal progress.

All this is before us and around us, if we would but note it. And this being so, the state of thought and of society, as few can fail to observe, is eminently calculated to afford those who disbelieve in the Supernatural, good opportunities of advance in the direction of negations. On the other hand, the presence amongst us of a sect of persons who call themselves "Spiritualists," and whose notorious words and works may be noted and criticized, is full of moment and importance. Spiritualism, when first it appeared and took shape, was treated with contempt. The facts urged by its supporters were denied; the manifestations almost universally disbelieved in. It was declared to be the work of acute knaves, or the offspring of idle and imaginative dreamers. Public writers treated it with scornful contempt. Reports of its strange proceedings and extraordinary developments were knowingly and deliberately suppressed. It was hastily hustled off the public stage, refused a hearing, and denied a defence. This policy, however convenient to its promoters, has failed. Sneers have not killed it. Its ideas and theories have been recently reduced to a formal system, while its votaries have increased to an extent scarcely credited. Christians and non-Christians, Roman Catholics, Church-of-England people and Protestants, have ranged themselves under its banner, and accept and propagate its views. To some the existence of spurious coin proves the value of the true; and the portents of these latter times are surely full of warning and value.

At all periods, it should be observed, certain classes of leaders of men's thoughts have succeeded in banishing the Supernatural from the field of human action. For example, Thucydides, representing the World exclusively in its natural aspect, did this. He had neither ear nor eye for the marvellous. In recent times, from the period of Locke to the beginning of the present century, a similar course was adopted by a very influential school of writers, remarkable for their careful dismissal of the miraculous, both from ken and consideration. To such, the World was a machine, wound up once for all by its Author, and needing no further application of that power which appeared to have spent itself, so to speak, in the act of creation. Like S. Peter's "scoffers," "walking after their own lusts," they practically declared, "since the fathers fell asleep, all things continue as they were from the beginning of creation."[1]

But, of course, such a state of thought could only be transitory. The universal convictions of man's conscience, and the most earnest desires of his heart, produced a reversion of opinion. The very dog-

---

[1] 2 St. Peter iii. 3, 4.

matic philosophers soon found themselves at sea. Reason and Imagination were starved, while the Understanding was profoundly flattered. This has so turned out, not once, nor twice, but continually. Scepticism has followed Superstition, and Superstition Scepticism. Wherever the Catholic Religion, having once been had, has been deliberately cast out and denied, there, as in Scotland at the present day, Superstition is more than ordinarily widespread and rampant. The Gnosticism and Manichæism of the early Christian era have reproduced themselves in later times; while Materialism has lived side by side with that Superstition which, on the surface, it seemed so necessary for the same Materialism to deny.

The following faithful account of the rise of the modern system of Spiritualism is borrowed from a contemporary record :—

"In December, 1847, a respectable farmer and his family, named Fox, settled in a house at Hydesville, a hamlet near Newark, in the State of New York. They were troubled from the first with noises, which in January, 1848, assumed the definite character of knockings, like that of a hammer. Two children, since so famous as the Misses Fox, felt something heavy, like a dog, lie on their feet when in bed, and one of them felt as if a cold hand were passed over her face. The knockings went on increasing in violence, and at length it was observed, on some occasion when Farmer Fox tried the windows to see if they could be caused by the wind, that the knockings exactly answered the rattle accidentally made by the moving sash. This suggested the idea of inviting the noises, or rather the beings who caused them, to reply by rapping, on repetition of the letters of the alphabet, to questions put to them. This was first tried at a place called Rochester, with which the family were connected, whence the term 'Rochester knockings' came into use. The experiment succeeded perfectly, and this was the origin of 'spirit-rapping,' which has since grown into a regular system. The neighbours being called in, the affair soon thickened and developed into a 'movement.' The rappings revealed a murder which had taken place in the house when in other hands. Public meetings were called, committees of ladies formed to examine the children, and prevent the possibility of deception. Similar phenomena began to show themselves in various parts of the country, and under yet more extraordinary conditions. Raps were heard on all sorts of objects—ceilings, tables, chairs, &c., and it was discovered that certain persons were better fitted than others to communicate with the spirits, to whom these noises were now attributed. Such persons were called *mediums*, a name with which the World is now sufficiently familiar, and when they were present, tables and chairs would move about and rise from the ground. Many other astonishing things became common, as drawing and music, executed under this strange influence, by persons who knew nothing of these arts."

As to its principles and policy, no better nor fairer exposition of them can be had than from the various publications which are so largely and generally circulated. From a pamphlet written with some system[1] by Mr. T. Grant of Maidstone, the following extracts, explanatory of the now formulated principles of Modern Spiritualism, are made:—

"TABLE OF MEDIA.

Outward.
1. Vibratory Medium.
2. Motive Medium.
3. Gesticulating Medium.
4. Tipping Medium.
5. Pantomimic Medium.
6. Impersonating Medium.

Inward.
7. Pulsatory Medium.
8. Manipulating Medium.
9. Neurological Medium.
10. Sympathetic Medium.
11. Clairlative Medium.
12. Homo-motor Medium.

Onward.
13. Symbolic Medium.
14. Psychologic Medium.
15. Psychometric Medium.
16. Pictorial Medium.
17. Duodynamic Medium.
18. Developing Medium.

Upward.
19. Therapeutic Medium.
20. Missionary Medium.
21. Telegraphic Medium.
22. Speaking Medium.
23. Clairvoyant Medium.
24. Impressional Medium.

"The *Outward* stratum includes all kinds of mediumship in which spirits act only on the physical

---

[1] "A Scientific View of Modern Spiritualism: a Paper read by Mr. T. Grant to the Maidstone and Mid-Kent Natural History and Philosophical Society on Tuesday, Dec. 31, 1872." London: J. Burns.

organism, first using simply the electrical or magnetic emanations from the medium and others in the room to produce movements of objects, or concussions called rappings, and to control matter in various ways; and secondly, using portions or the whole of the medium's body by direct action of spirits upon the bodily organs, the medium's spirit being more or less passive, and not taking part in the performance. . . .

"*Vibratory Mediumship.* I have often met with instances in my experience, and multitudes of persons are sometimes attacked together, with variations in accordance with individual character. The physical excitement and convulsive phenomena often witnessed at revival meetings are chiefly of this kind. . . .

"The *Motive Medium* comes next in order; he furnishes the magnetic power by which spirits are enabled to move tables and other material objects. . . .

"The third class is *Gesticulating Mediumship*, which appears to be a development of the vibratory. It is exhibited by the sect of 'Shakers' of the present day in the initiatory stage of their development, and was a form of mediumship common amongst the prophets of the Cevennes, the votaries of S. Vitus, and in most religious excitements.

"*Tipping Mediumship* follows next, and this again is a step in advance from the *Motive* mediumship, the movements of tables and other objects being so regulated by the intelligence of spirits as to produce telegraphic communications. . . .

"*Pantomimic media* belong to the fifth class; they are made, by the controlling or guardian spirit, to put themselves in various postures, so as to represent any peculiarity belonging to spirit-friends who are standing by, wishing to make their presence known and to communicate. Lecturers on electro-biology produce, to some extent, the same effects.

"The last in this stratum is the *Impersonating Mediumship*, which is a development from the Pantomimic. In this case the communicating spirit enters and takes full possession of the medium's body, whilst his own spirit stands aside."

The writer then passes on to consider what he terms the "Inward stratum," thus :—

"First we have *Pulsatory Mediumship*, in which the medium receives communications from spirits and answers to mental questions by means of pulsations, like tiny raps, on different parts of the body, or by sounds heard only by himself. These manifestations, although very convincing to the medium himself, afford but little satisfaction to anybody else.

"*Manipulating Mediumship*, which follows, is in fact Curative Mesmerism, in which, however, the will of the mesmeriser is strengthened and guided by spirits. Dr. Newton, of America, who visited Maidstone in 1870 and made several interesting and permanent cures, is a most remarkable and successful medium of this class, many of his cures having, indeed, all the appearance of miracles.

"In the next form of mediumship, the *Neurological*, the spirit impresses thoughts upon the brain, and the medium puts them into words; thus the communications partake of the peculiarities of the medium, and if the medium is impressed to write, he does so in his own handwriting and mode of diction and spelling.

"Next comes *Sympathetic Mediumship*, which is an extension of the Neurologic, but in which the spirits enter more intimately into sympathy with the medium. Both of these last are transitional forms of mediumship, and not very reliable until carefully developed.

"In *Clairlative Mediumship*, which succeeds in order, scenes of the past are clearly reproduced, or original scenes pictured to the mind, as in dreams and visions.[1]

---

[1] A remarkable example of this has been courteously given to me by Mr. Thomas Bosworth, of 198, High Holborn, as follows:—"Some seven or eight years ago there appeared in one of the newspapers a story to the following effect:—A commercial firm at Bolton, in Lancashire, had found that a considerable sum of money which had been sent to their bank by a confidential clerk, had not been placed to their credit. The clerk remembered the fact of taking the money, though not the particulars, but at the bank nothing was known of it. The clerk, feeling that he was liable to suspicion in the matter, and anxious to elucidate it, sought the help of

"The last of this Inward group is called the *Homo-motor* medium, one who is in perfect sympathy and under the complete control of one individual spirit only, who, in fact, appears to live a second life on earth in union with him."

And then he defines and discusses the "Onward stratum":—

"We begin with *Symbolic Mediumship*, in which the interior vision is opened by spiritual aid, and the medium sees in a vision the almost exact prefigurations of things which will occur at some future time, or which do in reality now exist, either in germ or in full or partial development.

"The second in this group, *Psychologic Mediumship*, is a very important form. A medium of this

---

a spirit medium. The medium promised to do her best. Having heard the story, she presently passed into a kind of trance. Shortly after she said, 'I see you on your way to the bank—I see you go into the bank—I see you go to such and such part of the bank—I see you hand some papers to a clerk—I see him put them in such and such a place under some other papers—and I see them there now.' The clerk went to the bank, directed the cashier where to look for the money, and it was found; the cashier afterwards remembering that in the hurry of business he had there deposited it. A relation of mine saw this story in a newspaper at the time, and wrote to the firm in question, the name of which was given, asking whether the facts were as stated. He was told in reply that they were. That gentleman who was applied to, having corrected one or two unimportant details in the above narration, wrote on November 9, 1874:—'Your account is a correct one. I have the answer of the firm to my enquiry at home now.'"

class is one who is in a condition to be impressed by a sympathetic spirit with any set of ideas which he desires to represent. It is sometimes done in a pictorial form, when the medium clearly sees and describes scenes which appear to the vision, such as the appearance and movements of an army, a landscape, a congregation in a cathedral, and so forth. . . .

"The *Psychometric Medium* has the power of feeling and correctly describing the characteristics of persons with whose spheres he or she is brought into sympathy or contact. The power is generally exercised by placing to the forehead, the perceptive region of the brain, anything which has been intimately connected with the person, as a piece of his hair, his handwriting, or a well-worn article of dress. Some will thus read a sealed letter or the mottoes enclosed in nuts. . . .

"*Pictorial Mediumship* differs from the Symbolic chiefly in the circumstance that the things seen and described by the medium do not in reality exist as material facts, but are only representations, prefiguring or bodying-forth a spiritual or psychical truth. . . .

"The next is the *Duodynamic Medium*, a word signifying two powers, he being capable of exhibiting two or more forms of mediumship at the same time. These compound media, maturely developed, are said to be comparatively rare.

"The last in this Onward stratum is the *Developing*

Medium, through whom spirits can very usefully assist in developing the mediumistic faculty in others. They have the power of harmonising the influences which affect them, and of rendering media passive to the action of the spirits who are seeking the control of their organisms."

As regards the " Upward stratum," the following definitions are given :—

" The *Therapeutic Medium* is one who effects the cure of many diseases through the sympathetic power of seeing and describing minutely the disorganized parts of the body, and directing the necessary treatment; sometimes the manipulating mediumship is added, when the medium not only sees the source of mischief, but also makes curative mesmeric passes at the same time.

" Next, we have the *Missionary Medium*, who is irresistibly compelled to go, without knowing why or whither, wherever the spirit guides him. Under this controlling influence, media have been made to travel nearly all over the civilized world, generally without purse or scrip, or any personal knowledge of the places; the spirits raising up friends and helpers at every step as they are required." Writing of a Missionary Medium known to himself, Mr. Grant adds the following :—" I am acquainted with a medium of this class in Maidstone, who is too weak in body to walk far in his ordinary state, yet, under this influence, he is often made to walk long distances without feeling fatigue, at the most unreasonable hours of day or night, and he has several times been instantaneously transported from one place to another, miles apart."

"Speaking mediumship," writes the author quoted, "is a most useful and instructive faculty. . . . . . . In most cases speakers have to be entranced, that is, their spirits have to be removed from the body for a time, in order to give the acting spirit full control; but when this has to be done the medium is but little advanced from the personating mediumship, which is one of the successive stages which a fully-developed speaking medium generally passes through. Many of our most celebrated and effective preachers and speakers have been, or are, really speaking media, under the guidance of spirits, without its being suspected or understood even by themselves. This is, indeed, 'inspiration.'

"The *Clairvoyant Medium* follows next in order, and is in advance of the telegraphic, because he is able to see the scenes that are actually transpiring at the time in another place, no matter how far distant.

"The *Impressional Medium* is generally one who has advanced through the neurologic, sympathetic, clairlative, and psychologic phases, and thus become so easily and thoroughly impressible by his guardian spirit that the medium appears to live a double life, the conditions and circumstances of both states of existence finding a ready expression through his organism at all times without his being entranced, the spiritual existence becoming as much as the physical his normal state." pp. 7—18.

The acts and deeds of Mr. Daniel Home, a Scotchman, and of the Davenport brothers, Americans, who figure very prominently as mediums in the authentic records of the spiritualists, are tolerably well known by report to many. From America, where the signs were first noticed, they came eastwards to England and the European continent, in which places the spiritual manifestations were even more remarkable than those which had occurred and been testified to in the West. Under the direction of a medium, people sat round a table, and by a silent invocation of spirits, by "willing"[1] that they should come, they came, and produced the following amongst other equally strange phenomena.[2] Large

---

[1] The term "willer" and "necromancer" are used as identical by Easterns as well as by the aborigines of New Zealand.

[2] There have been published "Rules to be Observed for the Spirit Circle," "framed under the Direction and Impression of Spirits," by Emma Hardinge, from which the following points are gathered. Firstly, there is a definition, and it is stated that "the Spirit Circle is the assembling together of a given number of persons for the purpose of seeking communion with the spirits who have passed away from Earth into the higher world of souls." A leading direction enjoins the inquiring votaries to "*Avoid strong* light, which by producing excessive motion in the atmosphere, disturbs the manifestations. A very subdued light is the most favourable for any manifestations of a magnetic character, especially for spiritual magnetism." "Strongly positive persons of any kind" and "the dogmatical" should not be admitted. Furthermore, these "Rules" contain the following :—

tables rose to the ceiling, floating in the atmosphere with a sort of undulating motion, and coming down again to the floor without noise; sprigs of flowers were torn off and presented to people by the spirit; accordions and other musical instruments were played without any visible hand holding or moving them; luminous stars and streaks of light appeared in various places, while "spirit hands" were seen and felt as palpably as mortal flesh and blood could be; answers to questions made, were given by a system of raps or by spelling out words on a child's alphabet placed on the floor. Thus conversations, sometimes sensible, but frequently trivial and absurd,[1] were held with the spirits summoned. Spirit hands, using material pens, ink and paper,

---

"Spirit control is often deficient, and at first almost always imperfect. *By often yielding to it, your organism becomes more flexible and the spirit more experienced;* and practice in control is absolutely necessary for spirits as well as mortals. *If dark and evil-disposed spirits manifest to you, never drive them away,* but always strive to elevate them and treat them as you would mortals under similar circumstances. Do not always attribute falsehoods to 'lying spirits,' or deceiving mediums. Many mistakes occur in the communion of which you cannot always be aware. *Strive for Truth,* but rebuke Error gently, and do not always attribute it to design, but rather to mistake, in so difficult and experimental a stage of the communion as mortals at present enjoy with spirits."

[1] The kind of communication made to those who first consult the spirits, is just of that nature calculated to allure the superficial, the frivolous, the uninformed, triflers, and seekers after novelties; and to lead them on to a more frequent intercourse and a deeper kind of communion.

wrote answers to queries; quoted verses from known authors, or put down original poems. In some cases the narratives published were anonymous, and only authenticated by witnesses who privately testified to the newspaper-editors their accuracy. But in some instances persons of repute and ability came forward in support of their correctness.[1] Dr. Gully of Malvern, for example, publicly testified that he had seen Mr. Home float about a room for several minutes, and guaranteed the accuracy of the facts set forth in a most remarkable fashion in an early number of the "Cornhill Magazine." A well-known clergyman of the High Church party in the Church of England, gives his testimony to the truth and strangeness of certain appearances and manifestations, in the following communication to the Editor of this volume:—

"I was staying in the north of England with the Rev. ——, in 1850. During my visit a well-known medium (at that period a clergyman of the diocese of London) spent the evening with us. Eight or ten other people were there at the same time.

---

[1] Dr. J. G. Davey, M.D., of Northwoods, Bristol, writes as follows:—"I have satisfied myself not only of the mere abstract truth of Spiritualism, but of its great and marvellous power for good, both on moral and religious grounds. The direct and positive communications vouchsafed to me from very many near and dear relatives and friends, said to be dead, have been of the most pleasing yet startling character." —*Report on Spiritualism*, p. 232. London: Longmans, 1871.

'Table-turning' was the subject of a long and animated discussion, in which those who accepted the facts and those who rejected them were about equally divided. There was nothing to be done, therefore, but to test the question. This was determined on. A circular table about four feet in diameter, of considerable size and weight, was used. Seven people sat round it, joining their hands on the table, and after conjointly *willing* that it should turn itself in one direction or be turned, for about twelve minutes, it began to vibrate strangely and then slowly to move. At first its motion was in circles, then it moved from side to side of the room with dash and rapidity. Afterwards it was strangely tilted on the other side. On one occasion later on, it rose several inches from the ground, and remained suspended in the air for nearly two minutes. As to the facts, no one could dispute them. Afterwards a variety of questions were put, to which the table replied by knocking on the floor. It was agreed beforehand that one knock should stand for 'No,' two for 'Yes.' An alphabet was produced, and words in response were spelled out. Some of the queries were trivial, some arithmetical, some momentous. The answers were usually accurate, sensible, and intelligible, but not always so. After questions had been put concerning the future state, heaven, hell, purgatory, the happiness of the good and the punishment of the wicked, a question was asked, 'Where did the spirit now answering dwell when on earth?' The name of a place in Devonshire was spelled out. This reply greatly interested a clergyman present, who some fifteen years previously had been curate in that county. It was followed by another :—'What was the name of the person whose spirit is here?' Then the table spelt out, by means of the alphabet, the name of a yeoman who had died impenitent and blaspheming at the period before referred to. This was sufficient for me," writes the above correspondent; "what I had heard and seen convinced me that necromancy was practised. I left the house, protecting myself by the sacred sign, convinced of the sin of the practice. And though I had been a spectator and not an actor, I made a resolution, which I have scrupulously kept, never to see nor sanction such proceedings again."

Another somewhat similar example is here recorded. A clergyman of the Church of England, intimately known to the Editor of this volume, supplies the following remarkable narrative regarding the action and authors of Spiritualistic manifestations :—" Being a perfect and total sceptic as to the supernatural character of so-called 'Spiritualism,' and believing that the results asserted to be produced by its votaries were brought about by prearranged trickery and the deception of confederates, I for a long time declined to be present at, or to take part in, a *séance*, though earnestly pressed to do so. However, circumstances led me to attend one in the year 1862, at a house in Notting Hill Square,

London, in the month of October. Prior to the operations, which were managed and conducted by a 'medium,' I was invited to examine both the room where the *séance* was to be held, and the table by which the operations were to be conducted. Conversations, held by a well-known spiritualist, were to be carried on, (by means of an alphabet, raps and knockings,) with the spirits who were presumed to be present, and who were declared to have miraculously moved the table round which, for some time, seven persons, including myself, had been sitting. The room was about ten feet in height, and in the centre was a gas chandelier of three lights, all of which were burning. During the sitting, after the table had made several most remarkable gyrations, tilting one side of itself upwards and downwards at an angle of at least forty-five degrees, at the command of the chief operator it slowly ascended from the floor to the height of at least seven feet, viz. the bottom of the pendent gaselier. Its plane having caused the lamp glasses to rattle by contact, the table then with a strange throbbing and vibration and slow movement began to descend. We had all removed our chairs, to give room for its ascent, and standing close to the walls around, saw it slowly come down to its place. I was so shocked and horrified at what I beheld, and now so firmly convinced that the remarkable actions we had witnessed were the result of the invocation and intervention of evil spirits, that I declined, in language most positive and unmistakable, to have any further part in such unlawful performances. When further attempts were made to obtain fresh manifestations, taking from my neck a small silver crucifix, which had been blessed by a high ecclesiastical dignitary, I made a mental act of faith in the Blessed Trinity, and holding the small crucifix in my closed hand, placed my hand clasping it on the table, saying mentally, '·If this be the work of evil spirits, may God Almighty, for Christ's sake, stop it!' The moment I did this, the table, which had been moving about strangely in several directions, and by varied singular motions, became suddenly and at once motionless. Nor could it be made to stir afterwards. Being perfectly convinced that such operations were of the nature of Necromancy, forbidden by the Church, as Scripture plainly testifies, I made an earnest exhortation to those in the room, after the last manifestation, not to cooperate in such deeds any further. Some maintained by rather blasphemous arguments that Spiritualism was destined to, and would soon, take the place of Christianity; and were kind enough to pity my ignorance, narrowness, prejudice, and sectarianism, to which I made no reply. I then left."

From another source (a well-known country gentleman in one of the midland counties) has been obtained a series of questions and answers which were put, given, and taken down in the year 1856, at a gathering at which the practice of table-turning and spirit invocation was tested by those whose conviction, in the main, regarding them, as the Editor is informed, agrees with that of the correspondents already quoted. Similar strange phenomena occurred on this occasion likewise :—

"Are you a Spirit who inhabited this earth? Yes.

How long have you been dead? No reply.

Have you been dead years? No.

Months? No.

Weeks? No.

Days? Yes.

How many? Five days.

Do you mean five days? Yes.

Did you live in this neighbourhood? Yes.

Did you know any at this table? Yes.

Will you point them out? Yes.

(It then crossed the room three times violently and stopped before three persons.)

Will you spell your name? Yes. R———— J————[1] (the way he always spelt it).

Are you happy? No answer.

Can we do you any good? No.

Was the Baptist religion true? No.

Will you spell the true religion? Yes—Saients.

Is there a middle state of souls? Yes.

---

[1] This person, whose name was most accurately given, had died five days previously. He was a servant on the estate, and had belonged to the sect of the Anabaptists.

Will the end of the World be soon? Yes.

Will it be the end of the World or the end of wickedness? The end of wickedness? Yes.

Will the World be destroyed by water? No.

By fire? No.

Will it be partly destroyed by fire? Yes.

Shall any of us see the Last Day? Yes.

In how many years? Twenty-five years.

Will the Last Judgment be then? No.

Will that be the Millennium? Yes.

Will Enoch and Elijah come again? Yes.

Will the Jews be restored? Yes.

Will Russia conquer England? Yes.

Will it be in the reign of Queen Victoria? No.

In the reign of her successor? Yes."

The testimony of Mr. Crookes, the discoverer of a new metal, and a Fellow of the Royal Society, may here be suitably recorded. Unlike some other so-called "scientific investigators," he is reported to have resolved upon a careful and thorough examination of the spiritualistic phenomena. He is said to have maintained originally that, even if the alleged facts were true, he might be able to explain them by some natural law. Accordingly he thoughtfully pursued his inquiries and investigations over a series of years, taking unusual care to render deception out of the question and impossible. The result has been given to the public in the "Quarterly Journal of Science" for January,

1874,[1] from which the following quotations are made:—

"The phenomena I am prepared to attest are so extraordinary and so directly oppose the most firmly-rooted articles of scientific belief—amongst others, the ubiquity and invariable action of the law of gravitation—that, even now, on recalling the details of what I witnessed, there is an antagonism in my mind between *reason*, which pronounces it to be scientifically impossible, and the consciousness that my senses, both of touch and sight—and these corroborated, as they were, by the senses of all who were present—are not lying witnesses when they testify against my preconceptions. But the supposition that there is a sort of mania or delusion which suddenly attacks a whole roomful of intelligent persons who are quite sane elsewhere, and that they all concur to the minutest particulars in the details of the occurrences of which they suppose themselves to be witnesses, seems to my mind more incredible than even the facts they attest" (pp. 77-78).

Under the heading of "The Phenomena of Percussive and other Allied Sounds," he makes reference to the raps and knocks of various kinds made and heard in different places, "in a living tree, on

---

[1] "Notes of an Enquiry into the Phenomena called Spiritualism, during the years 1870-73." By William Crookes, F.R.S.

a sheet of glass, on a stretched iron wire, on a stretched membrane, a tambourine, on the roof of a cab, and on the floor of a theatre," and where no known law, and no contrivance or trickery, could afford any clue to their cause. He then inquires whether the sounds thus heard are the result of some blind, irrational, hidden material force obeying the Laws of Nature. His conclusion, however, was that the varied phenomena being evidently governed by intelligence, a thinking being must have been concerned in their origination. "The intelligence," he maintains, "is sometimes of such a character as to lead to the belief that it does not emanate from any person present." The movement of heavy substances at a distance from the medium is then discussed, and Mr. Crookes thus writes:—

"On three successive evenings a small table moved slowly across the room, under conditions which I had specially pre-arranged, so as to answer any objections which might be raised to the evidence" (p. 84).

Again:—"On five separate occasions a heavy dining-table rose between a few inches and one and a half feet off the floor, under special circumstances which rendered trickery impossible. On another occasion a heavy table rose from the floor in full light, while I was holding the medium's hands and feet. On another occasion the table rose from the floor, not only when no person was touching it, but under conditions that I had pre-arranged, so as to assure unquestionable proof of the fact" (p. 85).

Once more:—

"On one occasion I witnessed a chair, with a lady sitting on it, rise several inches from the ground. On another occasion, to avoid the suspicion of this being in some way performed by herself, the lady knelt on the chair in such manner that its four feet were visible to us. It then rose about three inches, remained suspended for about ten seconds, and then slowly descended. At another time two children, on separate occasions, rose from the floor with their chairs, in full daylight, under (to me) most satisfactory conditions; for I was kneeling and keeping close watch upon the feet of the chair, and observing that no one might touch them" (p. 85).

Respecting another class of phenomena, said to be common enough with Modern Spiritualists, which appeal to the sense of sight, under the head of "Luminous Appearances," Mr. Crookes thus writes:—

"Under the strictest test conditions I have seen a solid self-luminous body, the size and nearly the shape of a turkey's egg, float noiselessly about the room, at one time higher than anyone present could reach standing on tip-toe, and then gently descend to the floor. It was visible for more than ten minutes, and before it faded away it struck the table three times, with a sound like that of a hard, solid body. During this time the medium was lying back, apparently insensible, in an easy-chair.

"I have seen luminous points of light darting about and settling on the heads of different persons; I have had questions answered by the flashing of a bright light a desired number of times in front of my face. I have seen sparks of light rising from the table to the ceiling, and again falling upon the table, striking it with an audible sound. I have had an alphabetical communication given by luminous flashes occurring before me in the air, whilst my hand was moving about amongst them. I have seen a luminous cloud floating upwards to a picture. Under the strictest test conditions, I have more than once had a solid, self-luminous crystalline body placed in my hand by a hand which did not belong to any person in the room. In the light, I have seen a luminous cloud hover over a heliotrope on a side-table, break a sprig off, and carry the sprig to a lady; and on some occasions I have seen a similar luminous cloud visibly condense to the form of a hand, and carry small objects about" (p. 87).

Two pages later on the following occurs:—

"I was sitting next to the medium, Miss Fox, the only other persons present being my wife and a lady relative, and I was holding the medium's two hands in one of mine, whilst her feet were resting on my feet. Paper was on the table before us, and my disengaged hand was holding a pencil.

"A luminous hand came down from the upper part of the room, and after hovering near me for a few seconds, took the pencil from my hand, rapidly wrote on a sheet of paper, threw the pencil down, and then rose up over our heads, gradually fading into darkness" (p. 89).

And then Mr. Crookes testifies that not only spirit-hands, but spectres or spirit-persons in their entirety, were seen:—

"In the dusk of the evening, during a *séance* with Mr. Home at my house, the curtains of a window about eight feet from Mr. Home were seen to move. A dark, shadowy, semi-transparent form like that of a man was then seen by all present standing near the window, waving the curtain with his hand. As we looked, the form faded away and the curtain ceased to move. The following is a still more striking instance. As in the former case, Mr. Home was the medium. A phantom form came from a corner of the room, took an accordion in its hand, and then glided about the room playing the instrument. The form was visible to all present for many minutes, Mr. Home also being seen at the same time. Coming rather close to a lady who was sitting apart from the rest of the company, she gave a slight cry, upon which it vanished" (p. 90).

In conclusion Mr. Crookes sets forth five current theories with regard to these and similar phenomena; one of which theories is clearly expressed in the following sentence. These supernatural manifestations, he asserts, some maintain to be "the actions of Evil Spirits or Devils, personifying who or what they please, in order to undermine Christianity and to ruin men's souls" (p. 96). Such a definition, it may be added, is in perfect accordance with ordinary experience, the testimony of Scripture, the action and teaching of the living Church, as well as a fulfilment of express and definite prophecies regarding "the latter days."

MODERN SPIRITUALISM.

CONTINUED.

"Superstition, in its grossest form, is the worship of Evil Spirits."—*John Henry Newman.*

"Let no man deceive you by any means: for that day shall not come, except there come a falling away first, and that Man of Sin be revealed, the Son of Perdition, who opposeth and exalteth himself above all that is called God, or that is worshipped. . . . . Whose coming is after the working of Satan, with all power and signs and lying wonders, and with all deceivableness of unrighteousness in them that perish; because they received not the love of the Truth that they might be saved. And for this cause God shall send them a strong delusion that they should believe a lie."—2 *Thess.* ii. 3-11.

"The greatest intellectual triumph that can be achieved by the Devil is gained when men are prepared to believe that he is not."—*Sermons, Rev. T. T. Lee* (A.D. 1796).

CHAPTER IX.

MODERN SPIRITUALISM.

(Continued.)

ORE recently the manifestations have been still further developed. From the "Spiritual Magazine" the following is quoted:—

"The *séance* was held by appointment. Our object being that of investigation, we limited the number to three, and, I must add, used every precaution we could think of to preclude the possibility of self-deception; we likewise guarded against any possible preparatory arrangement. Accordingly, we changed from the library to the dining-room. We were soon seated at a heavy square table. Twenty minutes passed without any manifestation; then came gentle raps, followed by the table being lifted, tilted, and gently vibrated. Then raps were heard simultaneously in different and opposite parts of the room.

At my suggestion, the lamp was partly turned down, when a cold current of air was felt to pass over our hands and faces. A pause ensued. The dining-room table leaf standing in the corner of the room then commenced to vibrate, and one of the leaves being taken from the stand, was passed between Mr. Home and the table at which we were seated. It was then raised straight up, and passing vertically over my friend, gently touched him; in passing over me, it struck me on the crown of the head, but so gently, that I could hardly realize it to be the heavy leaf of the dining-room table; the touch nevertheless caused the leaf to vibrate all but sonorously. I name this to prove how delicately balanced and suspended in the air the leaf of the table must have been to have produced the vibration. It then passed over to the right, touching my shoulders, and finally was placed upon the table at which we were seated. The distance the leaf was carried I compute at nearly twelve yards (allowing for the circuit made), and at an elevation of six feet. A small round table was then moved from the corner of the room, and placed next to my friend; and in reply to his question '*who it was*,' he received the answer, audible to us all, '*Pa, Pa,—dear—darling Pa.*' An arm-chair behind my friend, and at a distance of three yards, was raised up straight into the air, carried over our heads, and placed upon the dining-room table to my left, a voice clearly and loudly repeating the words, 'Papa's chair.' We then observed the wooden box of the accordion being carried from the extreme corner of the room up to my friend. In passing my right hand, I passed my hand under and over the box, as it travelled suspended in the air to my front. I did this to make sure of the fact of its being moved by an invisible agency, and not by means of mechanical aid. . . . . . . The accordion was then taken from Mr. Home, carried about in the room, and played. Voices were distinctly heard; a low whispering, and voices imitating the break of a wave on the shore. Finally, the accordion placed itself upon the table we were seated at, and two luminous hands were distinctly seen resting on the keys of the instrument. They remained luminously visible for from twenty to thirty seconds, and then melted away. I had, in the meantime, and at the request of my friend, taken hold of the accordion; whilst so held by me, an invisible hand laid hold of the instrument, and played for two or three minutes what appeared to me to be sacred music. Voices were then heard, a kind of murmuring or low whistling and breathing; at times in imitation of the murmur of the waves of the sea, at other times more plaintively melodious. The accordion was then a second time taken by an invisible power, carried over our heads, and a small piece of sacred music played,—then a hymn, voices in deep sonorous notes singing the hallelujah. I thought I could make out three voices, but my friend said he could speak to four. A jet of light then crossed the room, after which a star or brilliantly illuminated disk, followed by the appearance of a softly luminous column of light, which moved up between me and my friend. I cannot say that I could discern any distinct outline. The luminous column appeared to me to be about five to six feet high, the subdued soft light mounting from it half illumining the room. The column or luminous appearance then passed to my right, and a chair was moved and placed next to me. I distinctly heard the rustling as of a silk dress. Instinctively I put my hand forward to ascertain the presence of the guest, when a soft hand seized my hand and wrist. I then felt that the skirt of a dress had covered my knees. I grasped it; it felt like thick silk, and melted away as I firmly clenched my hand on it. By this time I admit I shuddered. A heavy footstep then passed to my right, the floor vibrating to the footfall; the spirit-form now walked up to the fire-place, clapping its hands as it passed me. I then felt something press against the back of my chair; the weight was so great, that as the form leaned on my shoulder, I had to bend forward under the pressure. Two hands gently pressed my forehead; I noticed a luminous appearance at my right; I was kissed, and what to me at the time made my very frame thrill again, spoken to in a sweet, low, melodious voice. The words uttered by the spirit were distinctly heard by all present. As the spirit-form passed away, it repeated the words, 'I kissed you, I kissed you,' and I felt three taps on each shoulder, audible to all present, as if in parting to reimpress me with the reality of its presence. I shuddered again, and, in spite of all my heroism, felt very 'uncanny.' My friend now called our attention to his being patted by a soft hand on his head. I heard a kiss, and then the words, 'Papa, dear papa.' He said his left hand was being kissed, and that a soft, child-like hand was caressing him. A cloud of light appeared to be standing at his left."

Another example, from the same publication, deserves to be put on record:—

"The first group of the manifestations (I use the term 'group' to mark the characteristic difference of the phenomena on each occasion,) occurred at a friend's house at Great Malvern. Those present had only incidentally met; and, owing to a prohibition being laid upon Mr. Home by his medical man against trying his strength, no *séance* was attempted. I name this as characteristic. Raps in different parts of the room, and the movement of furniture, however, soon told the presence of the invisibles. The library in which the party had met communicated with the hall; and the door having been left half open, a broad stream of light from the burners of the gas-lamp lit up the room. At the suggestion of one of the party, the candles were removed. The rapping, which had till then been heard in different parts of the room, suddenly made a pause, and then the unusual phenomena of the appearance of spirit-forms manifested itself. The opening of the half-closed door was suddenly darkened by an invisible agency, the room becoming pitch dark. Then the wall opposite became illumined, the library now being lit up by a luminous element, for it cannot be described otherwise. Between those present and the opposite and now illumined wall two spirit-forms were seen, their shadowy outline on the wall well defined. The forms moved to and fro. They made an effort to speak; the articulation, however, was too imperfect to permit of the meaning of the words to be understood. The darkening which had obscured the half-closed door was then removed, and the broad light from the hall lamp reappeared, looking quite dim in comparison with the luminous brilliancy of the light that had passed away. Again the room became darkened, then illumined, and a colossal head and shoulders appeared to rise from the floor, visible only by the shadow it cast upon the illumined wall. What added to the interest was the apparent darkening and lighting up of the room at will, and that repeatedly, the library door remaining half open all the while. The time occupied by these phenomena was perhaps five to ten minutes, the manifestations terminating quite abruptly."

A correspondent of the same serial gives the following facts :—

"On the 1st October, 1865, I attended a *séance* at 13, Victoria Place, Clifton, where the younger Mrs. Marshall, the well-known medium from London, was staying.

"I had previously prepared, as a test, a series of written questions inserted in a book and numbered consecutively; my wife, who was present, was by the usual method put in communication with the spirit of her mother, and the following are a few of the results. It is important to observe that no clue was given to the medium, or to the others present, as to the nature of the answer required, the questions being put in the following form :—'Will you answer the question No. 33?' &c., and as the answers were occasionally given in a different form from what was anticipated, though still quite correctly, these two facts taken together conclusively prove, as it appears to me, that the answers were neither the result of any knowledge on the part of the medium, nor any 'reflex action' from the mind of the interrogator.

"The spirit having been requested to answer the question numbered 33, viz. :—'Will you spell the name of the place where we lived when you left this state?' The reply, spelt through the alphabet, was 'Aust.'

"Question No. 34 having been put in the same manner, viz.:—'Where was your body buried?' The reply was, 'Saint George's.'

"No. 35.—'While your body was lying in the

coffin, was anything put in the hand?'[1] Reply, 'Yes.'

"No. 36.—'What was it?' Reply, 'A sprig of myrtle.'

"No. 37.—'By whom was it put there?' Reply, 'Thomas Bowman.'

"No. 38.—'Who else were present at the time?' Reply, 'Ann, Tommy and Mary Bowman Bryant.'

"Many other replies were given of an equally satisfactory character, but I must not further trespass on your space. I would merely remark that the answers in each case were quite correct, and that the events referred to occurred upwards of forty years since."

Again, Mr. James Howell, of 7, Guildford Road, Brighton, writes as follows in the "Spiritual Magazine" for November, 1867:—

"When I was at the Marshalls' last summer, a circumstance, unknown to anyone present save myself, was made known to me by unaccountable means. The name of a young lady who suffered and died from spinal complaint in the year 1843 was correctly spelled out, and the date of her death

---

[1] "The reader who has not been in the habit of attending *séances* should be informed that the peculiar phraseology of some of the questions is rendered necessary by the fact that if you ask the spirits, 'Where did *you* die?' or 'Where were *you* buried?' they will sometimes tell you that it was not *they* who died and were buried, but merely the external shell or material covering of the real man."—Note by the Editor of the "Spiritual Magazine."

given. I was most intimately acquainted with her. She was good, pious, and highly intellectual. To her I owe my knowledge of the French language, and my love of its literature. I was not thinking of her at the time; in fact, she was furthest from my thoughts; yet her name—a very uncommon one, you will admit—was given correctly, 'Aletta V——.' Now I am honest enough to confess that a million guesses would not have guessed that name. I was astounded and affected; for it brought back to my mind a rush of thoughts, happy and sad, of those evenings when I sat by her bedside listening to her sweet voice, and imbibing the original thoughts which sprang, not only from a well-stored mind, but one instinct with genius. Twenty-three years had elapsed from the time of her death; she had often promised to communicate with me from the spirit-world, if it was possible, and now that promise was fulfilled, even in the presence of others."

And once more, the same writer gives the following record of facts :—

"I paid a visit on Monday, July 2nd, to Mrs. Parks, of Cornwall Terrace, Regent's Park, then staying at 7, Bedford Square. Miss Purcell, the medium, went with me; and we three had some strong and wonderful manifestations. The table was turned about merrily, and once whirled round in mid-air. It became as animated as a living being; it even ran about when not a single being touched it. Knockings were heard all over the room; in chairs, in tables, under the floor, and along the wainscot. We had great trouble to keep the tables from being smashed.

"During the evening, the 'Blue Bells of Scotland' and '*Marlbrook s'en va-t-en guerre*' were knocked out on the table in a beautiful and correct manner, the table beating and dancing admirable time to each tune. At a previous *séance* a well-known tune was knocked out, and my wife was requested to dance, the spirits stating that the table should accompany her; but as we could not induce her to do so, we lost the promised *pas de deux* between a human being and a table. At my request the table also gave a series of knocks, viz. the footman's, the postman's, the tax-gatherer's, and the countryman's, which were perfect, and caused us much amusement. In one part of the room there appeared a silvery, bluish star, shining brilliantly. Mrs. Parks, strange to say, could not see it, but to the medium and myself it was clearly visible, at the same time too; and a brilliant member of the stellar creation it was, coming and going like those of the sky, when for a moment a veil of clouds passes over them."

The conviction that such acts and deeds are the work of evil spirits is put on record in the same serial, a formal organ of the Spiritualists, in the following narrative :—

"Mr. and Mrs. C—— attend a *séance* at which the spirit of 'a darling child' is manifestly present. They attend a second *séance*, and through the same medium they are confirmed in the conviction of the real presence of their child. Mr. C—— then finds that he is himself a medium, and forthwith he purchases a small table for the exercise of his power.

"His first experiment proves to him beyond a doubt that an intelligent being, though invisible, is with him; but he speedily begins to suspect that whatever the character may have been of the spirit which first manifested to him through another medium, this, which is now communicating through himself, is an evil spirit. On his 'wishing it to walk to the dining-room, it started at once.' He was struck by its heavy tread, 'so very unlike the footfalls of a young child,' and he exclaimed, 'This is *not* the spirit of my child, if so, I want no other manifestation.' Becoming more and more suspicious of the character of this particular visitant, he said, 'If thou art not the spirit of my child, march out of the house.' 'The table did, indeed, march, making a noise like the loud and well-measured footfalls of a heavy dragoon—literally shaking everything in the room.'

"This gentleman then adjured the spirit in a variety of forms, and asked if it was not a bad spirit? and it said, 'Yes!' Then he said, 'Accursed devil! by the living God I adjure thee to speak the truth! Has the spirit of my child *ever* been put in communication with myself or her mother through this or any other table?' The 'accursed devil' said, 'No, never!' Then, after similar assurances, Mr. C—— made up his mind to believe the devil; and he closed his experiments with an auto-da-fé, by breaking up and burning the table!"

Mr. Chevalier, who was the first witness called before the committee appointed by the Dialectical Society, gives the following personal version of this experiment, 20th July, 1869. He stated that he had had seventeen years' experience of Spiritualism, but it was not till 1866 that he commenced experimenting on tables. He obtained the usual phenomena, such as raps and tiltings and answers to questions. On one occasion, the answer which was given being obviously untrue, the witness peremptorily inquired why a correct answer had not been given, and the spirit in reply said, "Because I am Beelzebub." Mr. Chevalier, in continuation, said, "I continued my experiments until I heard of the 'Spiritual Athenæum.' About that time I lost a child, and heard my wife say she had been in communication with its spirit. I cautioned her, and yet was anxious to communicate also. I placed one finger on the table; it moved, and the name of the child was given. It was a French name. I told a friend of mine what had happened, but was laughed at by him; he however came, sceptic as he was. I placed one hand on the table asking mental questions, which were all answered. He then asked where my child went to school, not knowing himself, and the answer 'Fenton' was given; this also was correct. Frequently after this, I obtained manifestations in French and English, and messages as a child could send to a parent. At my meals I constantly rested my hand on a small table, and it seemed to join in the conversation. One day the table turned at right angles, and went into the corner of the room. I asked, 'Are you my child?' but obtained no answer. I then said, 'Are you from God?' but the table was still silent. I then said, 'In the Name of the Father, Son, and Holy Spirit, I command you to answer—are you from God?' One loud rap, a negative, was then given. 'Do you believe,' said I, 'that Christ died to save us from sin?' The answer was 'No!' 'Accursed spirit,' said I, 'leave the room.' The table then walked across the room, entered the adjoining one and quickened its steps. It was a small tripod table. It walked with a sidelong walk. It went to the door, shook the handle, and I opened it. The table then walked into the passage, and I repeated the adjuration, receiving the same answer. Fully convinced that I was dealing with an accursed spirit, I opened the street door, and the table was immediately silent; no movement or rap was heard. I returned alone to the drawing-room, and asked if there were any spirits present. Immediately I heard steps like those of a little child outside the door. I opened it, and the small table went into the corner as before, just as my child did when I reproved it for a fault. These manifestations continued until I used the adjuration, and I always found that they changed or ceased when the Name of God was mentioned. One night, when sitting alone in my drawing-room, I heard a noise at the top of the house; a servant who had heard it came into the room frightened. I went to the nursery and found that the sounds came from a spot near the bed. I pronounced the adjuration and they instantly ceased. The same sounds were afterwards heard in the kitchen, and I succeeded in restoring quiet as before.

"Reflecting on these singular facts, I determined to inquire further and really satisfy myself that the manifestations were what I suspected them to be. I went to Mrs. Marshall, and took with me three clever men, who were not at all likely to be deceived. I was quite unknown; we sat at a table, and had a *séance*: Mrs. Marshall told me the name of my child. I asked the spirit some questions, and then pronounced the adjuration. We all heard steps, which sounded as if someone was mounting the wall; in a few seconds the sounds ceased, and although Mrs. Marshall challenged again and again, the spirits did not answer, and she said she could not account for the phenomenon. In this case, I pronounced the adjuration mentally; no person knew what I had done. At a *séance*, held at the house of a friend of mine, at which I was present, manifestations were obtained, and, as I was known to be hostile, I was entreated not to interfere. I sat for two hours a passive spectator. I then asked the name of the spirit, and it gave the name of my child. 'In the

Name of the Father, Son, and Holy Ghost,' said I, 'are you the spirit of my child?' It answered, 'No!' and the word 'Devil' was spelled out."

Dr. Edmunds: "How were the names spelled out?"

Mr. Chevalier: "The legs rapped when the alphabet was called over. Mrs. Marshall used the alphabet herself, and the table rapped when her pencil came to the letters. My opinion of the phenomena is that the intelligence which is put in communication with us is a fallen one. It is the Devil, the Prince of the Powers of the air. I believe we commit the crime of Necromancy when we take part in these spiritual *séances*."

We obtain from these extracts, which might be multiplied thirty-fold from the authorized publications of the Spiritualists, some idea of the nature of their *séances* and proceedings. Our own statement at the outset has been more than justified as regards its moderation and accuracy from the examples provided in the extracts in question. "Necromancy" has been well defined to be "The art of communicating with devils and of doing surprising things by means of their aid; particularly that of calling up the dead and extorting answers from them." Now this, it seems clear, in one form or another, is precisely that which is carried on by a considerable and increasing section[1] of people in

---

[1] "There is scarcely a city or a considerable town in Continental Europe, at the present moment, where Spiritualists

America, in England, on the Continent, and elsewhere. It is practised mainly by persons who were such extreme Protestants in previous times that, having almost altogether denied the Supernatural, they have been reluctantly won over to a belief in it by communion with evil spirits. Father Perrone, the distinguished Jesuit, has calculated that upwards of two thousand treatises have been published in defence of the system of these manifestations during the past fifteen years. It has been pointedly remarked by an English clergyman, of those people who once, like the ancient Sadducees, rejected the idea of the existence of spirits, but who now have accepted the Spiritualistic theory, that " they have given up believing in nothing, and have taken to believe in the Devil."[1] And this epigrammatic saying is hardly too pointed. According to Perrone, the modern professors of divination frankly allow that the phenomena have passed through three phases. First, that of Mesmerism; secondly,

---

are not reckoned by hundreds if not by thousands; where regularly established communities do not habitually meet for spiritual purposes : and they reckon among them individuals of every class and avocation."—" Scepticism and Spiritualism." In a letter to the " Spiritual Magazine," dated May 4th, 1867, Judge Edmunds, of America, estimated the number of Spiritualists in the United States at ten millions. " In London, ten years ago," writes Mr. R. Dale Owen, there was but a single Spiritual paper; to-day there are five."—" The Debatable Land," p. 175. London: Trübner, 1871.

[1] The Rev. John Edwards, jun., M.A., Vicar of Prestbury, near Cheltenham.

artificial Somnambulism and Clairvoyance; and thirdly, Spiritualism, properly so called. He gives five reasons for maintaining his theory of diabolical agency with regard to the same. 1. From the nature of the phenomena. 2. From its effects. 3. From the manner in which Mesmerism operates. 4. From the malice and wickedness of the agent, who frequently utters anti-Christian and blasphemous doctrines; and lastly, 5. from the frank and candid admission of the mediums or operators themselves.

In most cases it may be safely assumed that evil spirits personify the souls of the departed. That such spirits are the deadly foes of man so long as he is in his period of probation, may, for all Catholic Christians, be also assumed. That such spirits, moreover, constantly represent the departed as continually desiring the hand of Death to fall upon their earthly friends, in order, as is implied or stated, that a future of unclouded light and everlasting happiness may speedily link them together, can be seen from a careful study of the records of Spiritualism. Some of the facts already set forth teach this. The principle that men, whether good or bad, righteous or unrighteous, will all be certainly saved, and be for ever hereafter in bliss, is the practical heresy[1] that Spiritualism in its theological

---

[1] "We do not, either by faith or works, *earn* Heaven, nor are we sentenced, on any Day of Wrath, to Hell. In the next world we simply gravitate to the position for which, by

aspect has most openly taught, and still continues to teach. "Spiritualism," writes Mr. William Howitt, a convert to it from Quakerism, "rejects the doctrine of eternal damnation as alike injurious to God and man. Injurious to God's noblest attributes, repugnant to the principles of justice, and unavailing in men as a motive to repentance. . . . Spiritualism knows that there are isolated passages in the Gospels and in the words of our Saviour capable of being made to bear an appearance favouring the doctrine of eternal punishment, but it knows that the original terms bear no such latitude, and when Christ says there is a state 'where the worm dieth not, and the fire is not quenched,' it admits the state, but denies that any of God's creatures will continue in that state a minute longer than is necessary to purge the foulness of sin and the love of sin out of their spiritual constitutions. Were the solution of this supposed difficulty much harder than it is, Spiritualism would place the love of God and the love of Christ, and all the great and gracious attributes of God and His Saviour—justice and truth and wisdom, and a charity more immeasurable than God Himself recommends to mankind, confidently and courageously against so horrible and senseless a doctrine."

---

life on earth, we have fitted ourselves; and we occupy that position *because* we are fitted for it."—"The Debatable Land," by R. Dale Owen, p. 125. London, 1871.

Now, though Spiritualism be ignored by the press, Universalism, its own offspring, is constantly and persistently maintained. Spiritualism also flatly denies the great Christian doctrine of the Resurrection of the body:—

"Spiritualism teaches, on the authority of Scripture and of all spirit-life, that there is no such thing as death: it is but a name given to the issue of the soul from the body. To those in bodies who witness this change, the spirit is invisible, and they only see a body which ceases all its living functions, has lost that intelligence which during so-called 'life' emanated from it, and lies stiff and cold, and to all appearance dead. But even the body is not dead. There is a law of life even in what is called dead matter, which is perpetually changing its particles and converting them into mere black earth and water, and hence into all the articles necessary for the physical life—corn, meat, wine, all foods, all fruits. The same law immediately begins to operate in the dead body, and, if unobstructed, speedily resolves it back into earth, and then forms this again into food and clothing and fresh enveloping forms for fresh human beings. The whole of the universe is in perpetual action, and the ever-revolving wheel of physical is subserving the perpetual evolution of spiritual life."[1]

---

[1] Howitt's "What Spiritualism has Taught," p. 8.

And again :—

"The Church of England and Spiritualism accord, but not in the doctrine of the resurrection of the body. The spirits all assert with S. Paul, that the body which rises from the death-bed is the spiritual body, and that the soul needs no other, much less an earthly body, in its spirit-home—that, in fact, nothing of the earth can ever enter heaven. That if the spirits of just men are *made perfect*, they can be nothing more, and no addition of anything belonging to this earth can add to their happiness, freedom, power, and perfection, but on the contrary. That so far from receiving at some indefinite and, probably, very distant period, their earthly bodies back again, they are continually, as they advance, casting off the subtler particles of matter that have interpenetrated their spiritual bodies."[1]

With regard to the influence of the Protestant Reformation on that temper of mind and habit of thought which have led sceptics and those whose faith has been overturned by the blasphemies of Calvin or the immoral principle of the Lutheran systems and their offshoots, to become votaries of Spiritualism, we cannot do better than put on record Mr. Howitt's deliberate judgment, expressed in language which, however painful to read in some parts, is at once forcible and pertinent :—

"By the denial of the intermediate states, the

---

[1] Howitt's "What Spiritualism has Taught," p. 10.

Protestant Reformers perpetrated a more monstrous outrage on the Divine justice, and more frightfully libelled the Divine mercy, than by the broadest stretch of imagination one would have thought it possible. By this arbitrary extinction of some of the loveliest regions of creation, by this wiping out of vast kingdoms of God's tolerance and goodness by the sponge of Protestant reaction, God's whole being was blackened, and every one of His eternal attributes dislocated and driven pell-mell into the limbo of Atheism. I say Atheism, for such a God could not possibly exist as this Protestant theory would have made Him—a God with less justice than the most stupid country squire ever established in the chair of magistracy; with less mercy than an inquisitor or a torturer with his red-hot pincers and iron boots. These atrocities were but the work of moments, but this system made the God of love and the Father of Jesus Christ sitting in endless bliss amid a favoured few, whilst below were incalculable populations suffering the tortures of fires which no period even of millions of years should extinguish, and that without any proportion whatever to the offences of the sufferers! All who were not 'spirits of just men made perfect' were, according to this doctrine, only admissible to this common hell, this common receptacle of the middling, bad, and the most bedevilled of devils! Never could any such monstrous, foul, and detestable doctrine issue from any source but that of the hearts of fiends themselves. None but devils could breed up so black a fog of blasphemy to blot out the image of a loving and paternal God from the view of His creatures. And yet the mocking devil induced the zealous Protestant fathers to accept this most truly 'doctrine of devils,' as an antidote to Popish error. As some glimmering of the direst consequences of this shutting-up of the middle states of the invisible world began to dawn on the Protestant mind, it set about to invent remedies and apply palliatives, and by a sort of spiritual hocus-pocus, it taught that if the greatest sinners did but call on Christ at the last gasp, they were converted into saints, and found themselves in heaven itself with God and the Lamb. This was only making the matter worse, and holding out a premium for the continuance in every sin and selfishness to the last moment. It was an awful temptation to self-deception presented to human selfishness. Millions, no doubt, have trusted to this wretched Protestant reed. . . . . . Yet common sense in others rejected and rejects the cruel deceit. A country poet, writing the epitaph of the blacksmith in my native village, expressed the truth on the Protestant theory of no middle regions :—

> 'Too bad for heaven, too good for hell,
> So where he's gone we cannot tell.'"

And now to conclude this portion of our subject, regarding which not a tenth part of the examples of " Spiritual" manifestations gathered has been given.

To have discussed the facts and theories provided on previous pages, would have occupied several chapters. Sufficient, however, is recorded to show that Spiritualism is directly antagonistic to the Christian Religion,[1] to point out the true character of many of the signs and wonders which exist in this nineteenth century, and which testify and witness to old and unchangeable truths. The ministry of

---

[1] "Spiritualism is avowedly opposed to the Christian Religion. 'The Creed of the spirits' is published in the shape of a little tract, one of those called 'Seed Corn,' which active agents love to distribute gratuitously wherever readers can be found, and these are its clauses: 'I believe in God'—' I believe in the immortality of the human soul'—' I believe in right and wrong'—'I believe in the communion of spirits as ministering angels.' Nothing more. Those well-intending persons, therefore—and we believe that among Protestants there are many—who go to *séances* out of curiosity, and who are sometimes heard to say that if Spiritualism be true it must therefore be right, should be warned that they are lending countenance to persons in whose writings the doctrines of the Trinity and the Divinity of our Lord Jesus Christ are emphatically denied—the Holy Ghost scoffed at in words too blasphemous for repetition, our Blessed Lady insulted, and the whole fabric of Religion attacked and undermined; and whether this is done by spirits who actually manifest themselves for the purpose of leading people astray, or by impostors who work upon the credulity of their audience, the thing can have but one origin, and that is the same as that of any other work by which the Arch-enemy seeks to close the heart of man against the True Faith. It is time therefore to use other weapons than that of ridicule against the baneful and, we fear, widely increasing delusion."—"Tablet," September 6, 1873.

"men and of angels in a wonderful order,"[1] the practice of exorcism, the facts of diabolical agency, possession by evil spirits, the sins of Witchcraft and Necromancy, are all more or less intertwined with the Divine Revelation which God has been pleased to give to man. But the Materialism of these latter days is blinding men's eyes, that they cannot see, and successfully destroying their faith in all that is beyond their cramped and narrow temporal range. Intellectual Paganism, and a positive disbelief in the distinct Nature of God, if not openly professed, is indirectly acknowledged; while the Faith of Pentecost, which for generations has regenerated the World, is cast aside as worn out, effete, and valueless. The possibility of miracle is derided; Providence is scouted as the fond dream of an exaggerated human self-love; belief in the power of prayer is asserted to be only a superstition, illustrative of man's ignorance of the scientific conception of law; the hypothesis of absolute invariable law, and the cognate conception of Nature as a self-evolved system of self-existent forces and self-existent matter, are ideas advancing with giant strides. Side by side with all this, however, stand the portentous phenomena referred to here. Let the existence of one course of such facts as those related be granted, and far more follows than the pure

---

[1] Collect for the Feast of S. Michael and All Angels, "Book of Common Prayer."

Materialist or the Positivist would for a moment allow. Yet none can deny the presence amongst us of such, evil in their essence and mischievous in their operations. The whole cycle represents the works of the Devil and his angels—works opposed at every step in theory by the Truths of Christianity, and in fact by the sacraments of the Church Universal. Man's highest and chiefest duty is to do the Will of the Most High: the practice of the Spiritualists, on the other hand (and let men lay the warning to heart), appears to be an intentional and systematic giving up of their wills to the evil one; an invocation of evil spirits for unlawful purposes, a "willing" for supernatural intervention in things which are not lawful, and a deliberate turning away from Him to Whom all power is given in Heaven and in Earth.

Appendix to Chapter IX.

Spiritualism and Science.

THE following Letter appeared in "The Times" newspaper a few years ago:—

"Sir,—Having been named by several of your correspondents as one of the scientific men who believe in Spiritualism, you will perhaps allow me to state briefly what amount of evidence has forced the belief upon me. I began the investigation about eight years ago, and I esteem it a fortunate thing that at that time the more marvellous phenomena were far less common and less accessible than they are now, because I was led to experiment largely at my own house, and among friends whom I could trust, and was able to establish to my own satisfaction, by means of a great variety of tests, the occurrence of sounds and movements not traceable to any known or conceivable physical cause. Having thus become thoroughly familiar with these undoubtedly genuine phenomena, I was able to compare them with the more powerful manifestations of several public mediums, and to recognize an identity of cause in both by means of a number of minute but highly characteristic resemblances. I was also able, by patient observation, to obtain tests of the reality of some of the more curious phenomena which appeared at the time, and still appear to me, to be conclusive. To go into details as to those experiences would require a volume, but I may, perhaps, be permitted briefly to describe one, from notes kept at the time, because it serves as an example of the complete security against deception which often occurs to the patient observer without seeking for it.

"A lady who had seen nothing of the phenomena asked me and my sister to accompany her to a well-known public medium. We went, and had a sitting alone in the bright light of a summer's day. After a number of the usual raps and movements, our lady friend asked if the name of the deceased person she was desirous of communicating with, could be spelt out. On receiving an answer in the affirmative, the lady pointed successively to the letters of a printed alphabet while I wrote down those at which three affirmative raps occurred. Neither I nor my sister knew the name the lady wished for, nor even the names of any of her deceased relatives; her own name had not been mentioned, and she had never been near the medium before. The following is exactly what happened, except that I alter the surname, which was a very unusual one, having no authority to publish it. The letters I wrote down were of the following kind:— y r n e h n o s p m o h t. After the first three—y r n—had been taken down, my friend said, "This is nonsense, we had better begin again." Just then her pencil was at e, and raps came, when a thought struck me (having read of, but never witnessed, a similar occurrence), and I said, 'Please go on, I think I see what is meant.' When the spelling was finished I handed the paper to her, but she could see no meaning in it till I divided it at the first h, and asked her to read each portion backwards, when to her intense astonishment the name 'Henry Thompson' came out, that of a deceased son of whom she had wished to hear, correct in every letter. Just about that time I had been hearing *ad nauseam* of the superhuman acuteness of mediums who detect the letters of the name the deluded visitors expect, notwithstanding all their care to pass the pencil over the letters with perfect regularity. This experience, however (for the substantial accuracy of which as above narrated I vouch), was and is, to my mind, a complete disproof of every explanation yet given of the means by which the names of deceased persons are rapped out. Of course I do not expect any sceptic, whether scientific or unscientific, to accept such facts, of which I could give many, on my testimony; but neither must they expect me, nor the thousands of intelligent men to whom equally conclusive tests have occurred, to accept their short and easy methods of explaining them.

"If I am not occupying too much of your valuable space I should like to make a few remarks on the misconceptions of many scientific men as to the nature of this inquiry, taking the Letters of your correspondent Mr. Dirks as an example. In the first place, he seems to think that it is an argument against the facts being genuine that they cannot all be produced and exhibited at will; and another argument against them, that they cannot be explained by any known laws. But neither can catalepsy, the fall of meteoric stones, nor hydrophobia be produced at will; yet these are all facts, and none the less so that the first is sometimes imitated, the second was once denied, and the symptoms of the third are often greatly exaggerated, while none of them is yet brought under the domain of strict science; yet no one would make this an argument for refusing to investigate these subjects. Again, I should not have expected a scientific man to state, as a reason for not examining it, that Spiritualism 'is opposed to every known natural law, especially the law of gravity,' and that it 'sets chymistry, human physiology, and mechanics at open defiance;' when the facts simply are that the phenomena, if true, depend upon a cause or causes which can overcome or counteract the action of these several forces, just as some of these forces often counteract or overcome others; and this should surely be a strong inducement to a man of science to investigate the subject.

"While not laying any claim myself to the title of 'a really scientific man,' there are some who deserve that epithet who have not yet been mentioned by your correspondents as at the same time spiritualists. Such I consider the late Dr. Robert Chambers, as well as Dr. Elliotson, Professor William Gregory, of Edinburgh; and Professor Hare, of Philadelphia—all unfortunately deceased; while Dr. Gully, of Malvern, as a scientific physician, and Judge Edmonds, one of the best American lawyers, have had the most ample means of investigation; yet all these not only were convinced of the reality of the most marvellous facts, but also accepted the theory of

Modern Spiritualism as the only one which would embrace and account for the facts. I am also acquainted with a living physiologist, of high rank as an original investigator, who is an equally firm believer.

"In conclusion I may say that, although I have heard a great many accusations of imposture, I have never detected it myself; and, although a large proportion of the more extraordinary phenomena are such that, if impostures, they could only be performed by means of ingenious apparatus or machinery, none has ever been discovered. I consider it no exaggeration to say that the main facts are now as well established and as easily verifiable as any of the more exceptional phenomena of nature which are not yet reduced to law. They have a most important bearing on the interpretation of History, which is full of narratives of similar facts, and on the nature of life and intellect, on which physical science throws a very feeble and uncertain light; and it is my firm and deliberate belief that every branch of philosophy must suffer till they are honestly and seriously investigated, and dealt with as constituting an essential portion of the phenomena of human nature.

"I am, Sir, yours obediently,
"ALFRED R. WALLACE."

The following Review, taken from the "Weekly Register" of August 1, 1874, will be read with interest :—

"The May and June numbers of the 'Fortnightly Review' for 1874, contain two remarkable articles by Mr. Wallace, the eminent naturalist. They are entitled— 'A Defence of Modern Spiritualism.' His aim in these is to prove the objective reality of its phenomena in the first instance, and then to show that the theory which explains them can be accepted by those who, like himself, entirely disbelieve in a Supernatural order. He points out that Modern Spiritualism is not in any way a survival or revival of old superstitions, but a completely new science. The facts upon which it rests have been known and noted from the earliest beginnings of history, but, owing to the influence of Superstition, were almost universally misinterpreted. Now, at last, these mists are clearing away. We have abundant materials upon which to work, and he looks forward with confidence to the establishment of a satisfactory scientific theory of a future life. Such a theory will be a truly regenerating influence, resting, not on arbitrary beliefs, but on established facts, and will, for the first time, make a true religion possible and a pure morality.

"At the close of the second essay, there is a sketch of the outline of the theory up to the point which it has reached as yet. Of course there is still much which requires to be explained and developed. The science is only in its infancy; but still its principles can be understood and appreciated. It is taken for granted that there are no spirits but human ones, these being the only spirits of which we can have any scientific knowledge. This being assumed, Mr. Wallace proceeds to give a short analysis of human nature, drawn from generalizations from the 'phenomena in their entirety,' and the communications of the spirits themselves. This is contained in four propositions:—

"1. Man is a duality, consisting of an organized spiritual form evolved coincidently with and permeating the physical body, and having corresponding organs and development.

"2. Death is the separation of this duality, and effects no change in the spirit, morally or intellectually.

"3. Progressive evolution of the intellectual and moral

nature is the destiny of individuals; the knowledge, attainments, and experience of earth-life forming the basis of spirit-life.

"4. Spirits can communicate through properly-endowed mediums. They are attracted to those they love or sympathise with. . . . But, as follows from Clause 2, their communications will be fallible, and must be judged and tested just as we do those of our fellow-men.

"From the acceptance of these propositions will result a far purer morality than any which either Religious systems or Philosophy have yet put forth, and with sanctions far more powerful and effective—'For the essential teaching of Spiritualism is that we are all, in every act and thought, helping to build up a "mental fabric" which will be and constitute ourselves more completely after the death of the body than it does now. Just as this fabric is well or ill built will our progress and happiness be aided or retarded. There will be no imposed rewards and punishments; but everyone will suffer the inevitable consequences of a well or ill spent life. The well-spent life is that in which those faculties which concern our personal physical well-being are subordinated to those which regard our social and intellectual well-being and the well-being of others; and that inherent feeling, which is so universal and so difficult to account for, that those latter constitute our higher nature, seems also to point to the conclusion that we are intended for a condition in which the former will be almost wholly unnecessary, and will gradually become rudimentary through disuse, while the latter will receive a corresponding development. This teaching will make a man dread to give way to passion, or falsehood, or a selfish and luxurious life—knowing that the inevitable consequences of such habits are future misery and a long and arduous struggle, in order to develop anew the faculties which had been crippled by long disuse. He will be deterred from crime, knowing that its unforeseen consequences may cause him ages of remorse, and his bad passions perpetual torment, in a state of being in which mental emotions cannot be drowned in the fierce struggles and sensual pleasures of a physical existence. And these beliefs (unlike those of theology) will have a living efficacy, because depending on facts occurring again and again within the family circle, and so bringing home the realities of the future life to the minds of even the most obtuse.' He asks us to 'contrast this system of natural and inevitable reward and retribution, dependent wholly on the proportionate development of our higher mental and moral nature, with the arbitrary system of rewards and punishments dependent on stated acts and beliefs only, as set forth by all dogmatic religions; and who can fail to see that the former is in harmony with the whole order of Nature—the latter opposed to it?' We cannot enter on the religious and moral questions which this brief survey of Mr. Wallace's theory suggests, but we wish to make some remarks on the 'facts' on which it is founded, and his treatment of them. The point that strikes one most in these articles is their evident sincerity. Mr. Wallace has become a believer in Spiritualism in spite of deeply-rooted prejudices against it, and he is anxious to deal thoroughly and impartially with all the facts connected with it as far as he can, without contradicting the first principles of his scientific creed. We can understand this limitation, for we, too, have first principles—first principles of which we are so certain that no seeming contradiction of them by facts could shake our belief. But the difference between our position and his is that our first principles are founded, not on facts of experience, but on a *belief* that God has spoken to us, and is speaking every day in the Church. Therefore, whatever God has revealed becomes to us as a first principle, which, *à priori*, cannot contradict facts, and which, as our knowledge increases, we more and more find experimentally to harmonize with them and explain them. But the whole of Mr. Wallace's theory is founded on the assumption that God does not speak—that He, and all that concerns Him, is unknown and unknowable to us; and this assumption rests, he would tell us, on facts—*i. e.* on his view of the order of Nature. Now, what we wish to point out is, that nothing which thus rests only on experience can, in any true sense, be called a first principle. It is merely a wide generalization, which may, any moment, be displaced by a still wider one. Mr. Lecky, in his 'History of Rationalism,' asserts that the evidence in favour of the reality of witchcraft would be irresistible, were we not convinced, on *à priori* grounds, that witchcraft is a delusion. Once Mr. Wallace fully shared this conviction, and found himself compelled, in his own words, to 'reject or ignore' all this evidence. Now, Modern Spiritualism has enabled him to accept all these, and other facts of a similar nature; and he expatiates on the relief he feels in being able to open his eyes to a whole host of things which he had hitherto been obliged painfully and laboriously to overlook. There is quite a string of them. Socrates' Demon, the ancient Oracles, all Miracles—those of the Bible, the lives of the Saints, and in the present day, answers to prayer, all the phenomena of Second Sight, Ghosts, and occult disturbances of all sorts. We cannot refer our readers to the articles themselves for the explanations, some of them very curious, of all these things. But we should like to ask whether it may not be possible that there may be some theory yet to be found still more comprehensive than Spiritualism,

and which may yield a still deeper joy and relief? The
one before us seems to us still to require a considerable
amount of reserve, to say no more, in dealing with some
of the facts. Professor Huxley objects to the amount of
twaddle that is talked by the spirits; but to this Mr. Wallace replies, very justly, we think, that it is no more than
we must expect, considering the mental and moral calibre
of the majority of mankind; and, consequently, of spirits,
who are not much improved by the mere fact of dying,
not to mention that of the spiritualists themselves; and
we know that the proverb, 'Like attracts like,' is especially applicable to mediums. But we confess that we
are surprised when we are told that 'sectarian' spirits
continue to maintain special dogmas and doctrines, while
yet quite unable to describe themselves as being in any
situation which at all corresponds to the orthodox teaching about a future life. We cannot understand what doctrines or dogmas could survive such a *désillusionnement*,
whether agreeable or the reverse, as Mr. Wallace's future
life would be to a spirit whose conceptions on the subject
had been moulded on any form of Christianity. Nor can
we conceive of any motive, except a diabolical malicious-
ness, which could prompt spirits to wish to keep up such
delusions among their surviving friends. And yet Mr.
Wallace explains the apparitions of Our Lady, &c., in
modern times, as being produced by spirits with strong
Catholic predilections, knowing that they would be very
efficacious in stimulating the cultus which they prefer.
And this is said without any moral comment whatever.
Also allowing, as he does, the reality of the apparitions,
though only of human origin, in the Bible and lives of
the saints, we are at a loss to see how he can say that
orthodox notions of heaven are never confirmed by spirits.
We should have said that it was precisely by them that

most of these had been originated, not to say confirmed. If his spirits are spirits, so are ours, and quite as worthy of credit. These are only a few of the difficulties on the surface of Sceptical Spiritualism. But we have already exceeded our limits. We will only add that we cannot but hope that, Spiritualism being so far an approach to truth that it admits an important class of facts which had lately been very much denied and ignored, may, by the difficulties which they raise, lead some minds to reconsider the position they have taken up with regard to the Supernatural. There is no bridge across the chasm which divides Faith from Unbelief, and yet in this World the edges are so close that it is but a step, and we pass from darkness into light."

SUMMARY AND CONCLUSION.

II.   P

" The Angel of the Lord tarrieth round about them that fear Him, and delivereth them."—*Psalm* xxxiv. 7.

" God sees at one view the whole thread of my existence, not only that part of it which I have already passed through, but that which runs forward into all the depths of Eternity. When I lay me down to sleep I recommend myself to His care; when I awake I give myself up to His direction. Amidst all the evils that threaten me, I look up to Him for help, and question not that He will either avert them, or turn them to my advantage. Though I know neither the time nor the manner of the death I am to die, I am not at all solicitous about it : because I am sure that He knows them both, and that He will not fail to comfort and support me under them."—*Addison.*

" Reverence the angels; shun the demons."—*Thomas Scott.*

CHAPTER X.

SUMMARY AND CONCLUSION.

EFORE a brief summary is made of the contents and purport of this book, an account of a most remarkable event which occurred at Oxford about forty-five years ago may be fitly chronicled. It will be known, in its general outline, by many Oxford men; and was given to the Editor in the month of June, 1854, by a member of Brasenose College, where it had occurred.

In the year 1829, a club, known as the "Hell-Fire Club," consisting of members of the university *in statu pupillari*,—formed in some respects on the model of that existing in the last century, which met at Medmenham Abbey,—was accustomed to meet twice a week at Brasenose College, in Oxford. Unbelief at that time is said to have taken coarser forms there than is the case now. Then it was less dangerous, because more gross and revolting. The members of the Club, however, were not unsuccessful in their imitation of the blasphemy, drunkenness and other sins which had so notoriously characterized the older society. They met twice a week, and each is reported to have endeavoured to outdo his fellow-member in rampant blasphemy and sceptical daring. The meetings were kept so private, and such judicious care was taken to preserve unity of thought and secrecy amongst the various members, that the College authorities, though partially aware of its existence, were said to be unable to interfere.

On the north side of the College runs a narrow lane, connecting the square in which Brasenose College faces that of All Souls, with Turl Street. Going towards the latter, on the left-hand side stands Brasenose, until it is joined by the north portion of Lincoln College. On the other side is the high garden wall of Exeter College. It is a dreary and dismal-looking thoroughfare at best; and especially so at night. The windows of Brasenose College are of a narrow Jacobean type, protected both by horizontal as well as perpendicular stanchions. The lower windows, being almost level with the street, were further secured by a coarse wire netting.

Towards midnight on a day in December in the year above-named, one of the Fellows of Brasenose College was returning home, when as he approached he saw a tall man apparently draped in a long cloak, and, as he imagined, helping to assist some one to get out of the window. The window belonged to the rooms of one who was reported to be a leading member of the Hell-Fire Club. Being one of the authorities of the College, he instinctively rushed forward to detect what he imagined to be the perpetration of a distinct breach of the rules, when (as he himself afterwards declared) a thrill of horror seized him in a moment, and he felt all at once convinced that it was no human being at whom, appalled and fear-stricken, he looked. As he rushed past he saw the owner of the rooms, as he conceived, being forcibly and strugglingly dragged between the iron stanchions. The form, the features,[1] horribly distorted and stamped with a look of indescribable agony, were vividly before him; and the tall figure seemed to hold the frantic struggler in a strong grasp.

He rushed past, round to the chief entrance, knocked at the gate, and then fell to the ground in a swoon. Just as the Porter opened it, there rose a cry from a crowd of men trooping out from a set of rooms immediately to the right of the Porter's lodge. They were members of the notorious Hell-Fire Club. In the middle of a violent speech, as profane as it is said to have been blasphemous, and with a frightful imprecation upon his lips, a chief

---

[1] "The soul has a kind of body of a quality of its own." —Tertull. cont. Marc. lib. v. cap. xv.

speaker (the owner of the rooms) had suddenly broken a blood vessel, and was then lying dead on the floor.

The club in question, it is reported, never met again.[1]

So much on this point. A few words are perhaps needed upon another. It may be held by some that what has already been written on Witchcraft and Necromancy is a melancholy instance of grovelling superstition on the part of its Author.[2] Be it so. He is quite ready to avow his

---

[1] This account is current, with slender and unimportant variations, at Oxford; or at all events *was* current in my days there (A.D. 1850-1854), and on what could not be regarded as other than good authority. One version is already in print—that given by Mr. William Maskell, at pp. 108-112 of his curious and interesting book, "Odds and Ends," London, 1872. He seems to imply that it was the late Archdeacon of Cleveland, the Ven. Edward Churton, who saw the spectral apparitions in Brasenose Lane; but the Archdeacon belonged to Christ Church, and, as his son, the Rev. W. R. Churton, of Cambridge, informs me, was not resident at Oxford at the time of the occurrence. More probably it was the Archdeacon's brother, the Rev. T. T. Churton, sometime Fellow of Brasenose.

[2] As to the universality of the belief in Witchcraft, the reader may consult Herder's "Philosophy of History," bk. viii. ch. 2. And as regards the convictions of some of the leading minds of Europe in times past on the subject, Mr. Leckey in his "History of Rationalism" (vol. i. p. 66), makes the following candid admission: "It is, I think, impossible to deny that the books in defence of the belief are not only far more numerous than the later works against it, but that they also represent far more learning, dialectic skill, and even

entire belief in the express statements of Holy Scripture, and in the general Christian tradition and teaching on the subject itself and all that is necessarily involved in it. Those who believe in the existence of angels, "the glorious battalions of the living God," and who frankly accept as truth the various records of Holy Scripture, in which their ministry to mankind is set forth, will likewise believe that S. Peter's exhortation to the Early Christians did not simply embody a sentiment but declared a fact, when he wrote: "Be sober, be vigilant, because your adversary the Devil, as a roaring lion, walketh about, seeking whom he may devour."[1]

---

general ability. For many centuries the ablest men were not merely unwilling to repudiate the superstition; they often pressed forward earnestly and with the most intense conviction to defend it. Indeed, during the period when Witchcraft was most prevalent there were few writers of real eminence who did not, on some occasion, take especial pains to throw the weight of their authority into the scale. Thomas Aquinas was probably the ablest writer of the thirteenth century, and he assures us that diseases and tempests are often the direct acts of the devil; that the devil can transport men at his pleasure through the air; and that he can transform them into any shape. Gerson, the Chancellor of the University of Paris, and, as many think, the author of 'The Imitation,' is justly regarded as one of the master intellects of his age; and he, too, wrote in defence of the belief. Bodin was unquestionably the most original political philosopher who had arisen since Machiavelli, and he devoted all his learning and acuteness to crushing the rising scepticism 'on the subject of witches.'"

[1] 1 S. Peter v. 8.

That the pagan nations owning and serving the Prince of this World, and being supernaturally served by him in return, actively practised magic at the time of our Blessed Saviour's first coming, is generally allowed. And that the Christian writers of early times, more particularly S. Gregory Thaumaturgus, admitted the reality and force of the sorcerers' incantations and powers, is abundantly evident from their words and reasoning. The case of the damsel of Thyatira, "possessed with a spirit of divination," who "brought her masters much gain by soothsaying," clearly establishes this point; and so does the apostle's authoritative action :—" Paul, being grieved, turned and said to the spirit, I command thee in the Name of Jesus Christ to come out of her. And he came out the same hour." [1]

When, three centuries after the Day of Pentecost, the Church of God commenced numbering up her earliest triumphs, the soothsayers, the diviners, and the dealers with evil spirits began to experience her righteous and beneficent power. Constantine, urged to action by those who sat in the seats of the apostles, formally sanctioned the condemnation of magicians; but of course under Julian the Apostate, magic rites were not only still commonly in vogue, but were publicly patronized. Later on, Valentinian re-enacted the laws of Constantine; and

---

[1] Acts xvi. 16-18.

under Theodosius the severest penalties were likewise enforced against the practice of magic; and, in truth, against every phase of pagan worship. But a general belief in sorcery and divination remained powerful and active long after the supreme and glorious victory of Christianity in the sixth century; and the manner in which the authorities of the Christian Church met the belief, and, by Sacraments and Sacramentals, aided the faithful to withstand the legions of the Devil and his human allies, is perfectly familiar to the student of history.

The well-known conviction that demons had appeared to mankind under the names of sylvans, gnomes, and fauns was common enough amongst the Romans prior to the revelation of Christianity; while the conviction that these demons had sometimes made women the object of their passion was arrived at by many. Justin Martyr and S. Augustine of Hippo[1] seem to imply something of the sort; and marriage or commerce with demons was a charge frequently made against witches, even from the earliest times.[2] It was said that these demons owned a remarkable attachment to women with beautiful hair,—a belief possibly founded on the passage in S. Paul's First Epistle to the Corinthians,[3] in which he exhorts women to cover their

---

[1] Apologia, cap. v.   De Civit. Dei, lib. xv. cap. xxiii.
[2] 1 Cor. xi. 10.   [3] Ibid. xi. 15.

heads "because of the angels." In the middle ages the intercourse of philosophers belonging to certain secret societies with sylphs and salamanders was also believed by many:[1] and, later on, the study of astrology, with its fatalistic theories, and the restoration of the heresies of the Manichees, served to aid in more systematically formulating that belief in witchcraft and the supernatural which was for centuries so universal, and which never could have become so without a sure and solid substratum of fact and truth.

Again, it is impossible to believe that the sor-

---

[1] Luther, following the current tradition of his day, believed that the Devil could beget children on the bodies of women; and declared that he himself had personally come across, and was well acquainted with, one of the Devil's offspring. So too did Erasmus believe the fact of such generation. It is a tradition in the Catholic Church, that the last and great Antichrist—the final Antichrist—may be born of such an alliance. Of course Mahomet was *a* great Antichrist; for though he borrowed certain Christian features and adopted many Jewish notions and Rabbinical traditions in his system, yet he plainly and undoubtedly fulfilled the prophetic statement of S. John the Divine—"*He is Antichrist, who denieth the Father and the Son.*" (1 S. John ii. 22.) Mahomet's great and leading heresy is expressed in the following dogmatic assertion of the Koran: "*God neither begetteth nor is begotten.*" Now no system has more pertinaciously, successfully, and for so long a time opposed Christianity than Mahometanism—not even Arianism. But modern "Liberalism," so called, as still developing amongst ancient Christian nations, promises even to outstrip the system of Mahomet, and to be as blighting and baneful in its results.

cerers of the Oriental nations have been and are impostors. As regards those of modern Egypt, Mr. Lane, in his interesting volume upon that country,[1] appears to have settled the question by expressing his conviction of the truth and reality of their supernatural performances. And similar conclusions have reluctantly but most certainly been arrived at by those who, with some knowledge and reasonable powers of observation, have witnessed the acts and deeds of the Eastern dealers with evil spirits.

With reference to Egypt, Mr. Lane's statement on the subject stands thus:—

"A few days after my arrival in this country my curiosity was excited on the subject of magic by a circumstance related to me by Mr. Salt, our consul-general. Having had reason to believe that one of his servants was a thief, from the fact of several articles of property having been stolen from his house, he sent for a celebrated Maghrabee magician, with a view of intimidating them, and causing the guilty one, (if any of them were guilty,) to confess his crime. The magician came, and said that he would cause the exact image of the person who had committed the thefts to appear to any youth not arrived at the age of puberty; and

---

[1] "An Account of the Manners and Customs of the Modern Egyptians." By E. W. Lane. 5th edition. London: 1860.

desired the master of the house to call in any boy whom he might choose. As several boys were then employed in a garden adjacent to the house, one of them was called for this purpose. In the palm of this boy's right hand, the magician drew with a pen a certain diagram, in the centre of which he poured a little ink. Into this ink he desired the boy steadfastly to look. He then burned some incense, and several bits of paper inscribed with charms; and at the same time called for various objects to appear in the ink. The boy declared that he saw all these objects, and, last of all, the image of the guilty person; he described his stature, countenance, and dress; said that he knew him; and directly ran down into the garden, and apprehended one of the labourers, who, when brought before the master, immediately confessed that he was the thief."—P. 267.[1]

The performers themselves maintain, that they have been instructed in the art by those who have traditionally received the knowledge step by step, and period by period, from the old "magicians of Egypt;" and some frankly allow, that they themselves are constantly attended and waited on by a familiar spirit, demon, or genius, who actively aids them in their performances, and who is, under certain circumstances, always prepared to do their bidding.

---

[1] See the whole of this chapter, which is full of information and interest. It gives a record of several other similar examples.

These genii, or "Ginn" as they are called in Egypt, "are said to be of pre-Adamite origin, and in their general properties," remarks Mr. Lane, "are an intermediate class of beings between angels and men, but inferior in dignity to both, created of fire, and capable of assuming the forms and material fabric of men, brutes, and monsters; and of becoming invisible at pleasure. They eat and drink, propagate their species (like or in conjunction with human beings,) and are subject to death." . . . . "The Ginn," continues Mr. Lane, "are supposed to pervade the solid matter of the earth, as well as the firmament, where, approaching the confines of the lowest heaven, they often listen to the conversation of the angels respecting future things, thus enabling themselves to assist diviners and magicians."—P. 222.

In the twentieth chapter of his interesting and attractive volume, he writes:—"I have met with many persons among the more intelligent of the Egyptians who condemn these modern Psylli as impostors, but none who has been able to offer a satisfactory explanation of the most common and most interesting of their performances."—P. 383.

In another part of the book Mr. Lane concludes his chapter on "Magic" thus:—"Neither I nor others have been able to discover any clue by which to penetrate the mystery."[1]

---

[1] In No. 117 of the "Quarterly Review," there is a criticism

So likewise as regards India,[1] it is impossible to set aside the facts, which are testified to not by one but by hundreds, as to the supernatural powers of the jugglers there. Identical in kind with the performances of the magicians of Egypt before Pharaoh and in the presence of Moses and Aaron, recorded in the Book of Exodus, the secret of the following "tricks" (familiar to any one who has been in India) has been handed down from father to son from the most remote ages; and we have no reason to doubt that the source of the power by which these acts are done is one and the same.

For instance:—The juggler, giving one of the spectators a coin to hold as securely as possible within his hands, after pronouncing incantations in a monotonous voice for some minutes, suddenly stops, still keeping his seat, makes a rapid motion with his right hand, as if in the act of throwing something at the person holding the coin, at the same time breathing with his mouth upon him. Instantaneously the hands of the person taking part in the performance are suddenly distended, while a horrible sensation of holding something cold and

---

on Mr. Lane's account of these necromancers; but the facts recorded by him are neither satisfactorily accounted for nor successfully explained away.

[1] My brother-in-law, Captain Ostrehan, of the Bombay Staff Corps, Sir Alfred Slade, Bart., and the Rev. Dr. Dunbar, chaplain to Bishop Claughton, have furnished me with remarkable examples of the power of Oriental necromancers.

disagreeable and nasty, is immediately felt, forcing him to cast away the contents of his palms, which, to the horror and disgust of uninitiated persons, turns out to be, not the coin which before was there, but a live snake coiled up! The juggler then rises, and catching the snake, which is now crawling and wriggling on the ground, takes it by the tail, opens his mouth wide, and allows the snake to drop into it. With deliberation he appears by degrees to swallow it, until the whole, tail and all, completely disappears. He opens his mouth for the spectators to investigate; but nothing is to be seen, neither does the snake appear again.

Here is another instance:—A juggler will be brought to act before, perhaps, many hundreds of people, of all ages, degrees, and religions, including the soldiery of a garrison, in the public yard of a barrack. A guard of soldiers will be placed around him, to prevent either trickery or deception on his part, or interruption from the spectators. A little girl, about eight or nine years old, accompanies the man, who is also provided with a tall, narrow basket, three or four feet high, little more than a foot in width, and open all the way up. The juggler, after some altercation with the child, pretends to get angry, and lashing himself into a fury, seizes hold of the child, and inverts the basket completely over her. Thus placed completely at his mercy, and in spite of her screams and entreaties, he draws his sword, and fiercely plunges it down into the basket, and brings it out dripping with blood—or what apparently is such. The child's screams become fainter and fainter, as again and again the sword is thrust through the basket; and at length they gradually cease, and everything is still. Then follows a critical moment for the supposed murderer: and the exertions of the guard scarcely serve to save him from the excited soldiery. When order is at length obtained, however, the man, raising his bloody sword for an instant, strikes the basket with it, which falls, and reveals—not a murdered child weltering in blood, but an empty space, with no vestige left of the supposed victim. In a few moments the identical little girl comes rushing—from whence no one can tell—to the feet of the performer, with every sign of affection, and perfectly unhurt. Be it observed that these performances commonly take place in India in places where it is impossible for any contrivances or trap-doors to exist, in the centre of court-yards at the various military stations, and before innumerable witnesses.

Again: in Corea and China the practice of Necromancy is said to be almost universal. An intelligent modern writer upon China gives an account, in the following passage, of one mode in which questions are put, and answers obtained, by a kind of divination:—Written communications from spirits are not unfrequently sought for in the following manner: after the presence and desired offices of some spirit are invoked, "two or more persons support with their hands some object to which a pencil is attached in a vertical position, and extending to a table below covered with sand. It is said that the movements of the pencil, involuntary as far as the persons holding it are concerned, but governed by the influences of spirits, describe certain characters which are easily deciphered, and which often bring to light remarkable disclosures and revelations. Many who regard themselves as persons of superior intelligence are firm believers in this mode of consulting spirits."[1]

Here, as illustrating the common principles and course of action which are adopted and followed in all parts of the World by those who seek information by forbidden means, the following may be set forth :—

There is a dreary-looking House in one of the London Squares which is reported to be haunted. And certainly this opinion, as the Editor can testify from a careful personal enquiry, is tolerably current in the neighbourhood. A Lady, curious about the fact, was present on an occasion when certain inquiries were made regarding this House by means of " Planchette,"—the instrument just referred to as so commonly used in China. It is a small board, in shape like a heart, which is made to

---

[1] Nevins' " China and the Chinese," p. 167. New York, 1868.

run on two wheels or castors, and a hole is provided for a pencil so to be placed with its point downward as that, when put upon a sheet of white paper the point may just touch the surface. After the usual invocation or incantation (or whatever it be), the persons who practise modern divination place their hands on the board. Questions are put, and answers given. No one touches the pencil, but the board is so guided, as the Necromancers and Spiritualists assert, that the pencil is made to write intelligible answers to expressed (and sometimes to mere mental) queries. The following, printed *verbatim et literatim*, are in the handwriting of the lady who witnessed them put and responded to, and are given as a fair specimen of this mode of divination, now so generally practised in England:—

Is any house haunted in B—— Square? Yes.

What killed the two people in the haunted room? Fright.

What frightened them? Spirits.

What kind of spirits? Yourself.

How could any one be afraid of me? Without your body.

Did they see them? Spirits not visible.

How did they know they were there? Thought they saw them.

Did they make them feel them? No.

Then how did the spirits make themselves known—by what means? Mesmeric.

Were you ever there? No.

Why do those spirits haunt that house? Murder was committed there.

Who was murdered, a man or a woman? A woman.

What was the name of the woman? (Writing not intelligible.)

Who murdered her? (Writing not intelligible.)

Is he alive or dead? Dead.

Is it the woman's spirit, or the man's, who haunts the house? Both.

Was the man hung? No.

Was the murder found out while he lived? No.

Are you a bad spirit? Bad.

Is it what the Bible calls "divination" to consult you in this way? Yes.

Is it displeasing to God? Perhaps.

Is it wrong? You know.

It is only right to add that those who made and obtained the foregoing intelligible responses to intelligible questions, for good and sufficient reasons came to hold such practices to be unlawful and wicked, and threw the instrument by which they had been given into the Thames.

On this subject, and all its details, no words of warning could be more forcible than the following, which are quoted, in the hope that some who may have been thoughtlessly induced to adopt the practices of Modern Spiritualism, may be led at once to desist from the same:—

"Although good and evil spirits possess a powerful influence in the government of the World, yet it is strictly forbidden, in the divine laws of the Old and New Testament, to seek any acquaintance with them, or to place ourselves in connection with and relation to them; and it is just as little permitted for citizens of the world of spirits visibly to manifest themselves to those who are still in the present state of existence, without the express command or permission of the Lord. He, therefore, that seeks intercourse with the invisible world sins deeply, and will soon repent of it; whilst he that becomes acquainted with it, without his own seeking and by Divine guidance, ought to beg and pray for wisdom, courage, and strength, for he has need of all these; and let him that is introduced into such a connection, by means of illness, or the aberration of his physical nature, seek by proper means to regain his health, and detach himself from intercourse with spirits."[1]

Yet, with many, and an increasing number, it is to be feared such advice is wholly unheeded. For more than five-and-twenty years the subject of Modern Spiritualism has been under discussion in England, and the facts on which it has been founded have been before the World; but "having eyes men see not, and having ears they hear not." Or, guided

---

[1] "Theory of Pneumatology," by J. H. Jung-Stilling, pp. 136-137. London: Longmans, 1834.

by the superficial opinions of those whose one-eyed Materialism tinges so many of their hap-hazard theories, they put aside a consideration of the astonishing phenomena of the system of Spiritualism, and absolutely deny their existence.[1] The age is shallow in its very incredulity. The wisdom of the World is foolishness indeed.

---

[1] Dr. Sexton in his "Defence of Modern Spiritualism" (London: J. Burns), a tractate written with ability and frankness, remarks that "it is too late in the day to sneer at this matter with a sort of self-complacency, which seems to say, 'You are a poor deluded creature: behold my superior wisdom; I don't believe in such nonsense.' Here are the facts, and we demand in the true spirit of Science to know what is to be done with them. If you have any theory by which they can be explained, let us hear it, in order that we may judge of its merits; if you have not, we are all the more justified in clinging to our own." And, again, referring to the inquiries of a certain Dr. Hare in America, he writes:—
"The question with Dr. Hare was—Did the phenomena occur, and, if so, were they produced by the direct action of those persons in whose presence they took place? The nonsensical notions mooted by unscientific opponents, and which are still urged with as much gravity as though they had been made the subject of mathematical demonstration, that electricity, magnetism, odic, or psychic forces are the agents by which the manifestations are produced, he knew well enough could not bear a moment's investigation. Electricity cannot move tables, nor in fact act at all without cumbrous apparatus. Magnetism cannot give intelligent responses to questions, and odic force and its twin brother psychic are probably as imaginary as the philosopher's stone; and even if their existence could be proved beyond the shadow of a doubt, they could not in the slightest degree help us to the solution of the great problem of the cause of the phenomena designated Spiritual."

When it is too late, when thousands upon thousands have become the active votaries of Spiritualism, perhaps the bishops and clergy of the Church of England may wake up to some realization of the enormous influence for evil,[1] both dogmatic and moral, which this diabolical system cannot do other than secure, and lift their testimony against it. Mahometanism is not more directly anti-

---

[1] A thoughtful writer, and one who is evidently far-seeing and awake to the danger, recently made the following pertinent remarks in the *Church Review* :—

" The presence of Superstition is always the sign of a wandering from the true path ; the *excess* of Superstition almost invariably the precursor of great intellectual and religious changes, if not absolute convulsions. Before the great crash of Paganism the necromancers and practisers of curious arts were carrying on an unusually brisk trade among the Romans. We all know how prevalent was the belief in witches, wizards, and astrology at the time immediately preceding the (so-called) Reformation. Before the French Revolution the sect founded by Cagliostro and Lorenza Feliciani, which professed a knowledge of the ancient arts of the Egyptians, found great numbers of followers. And have we not a sign of a national mental crisis in our own day in the prevalence of ' Spiritualism,' which is the form which necromancy at present takes ? There may be many people who are utterly unaware how large a number of their fellow-countrymen, and especially of their countrywomen, believe in Spiritualism, and attend *séances*. Those who do so are not usually very fond of parading their belief, because they have a lurking suspicion that they may get laughed at ; but this very reserve makes the bond between the votaries of Spiritualism so much the stronger. It is no exaggeration to say that the practice of dealing with familiar spirits is on the increase in Great Britain at the present moment." (A. D. 1873.)

christian. Yet the numbers of those who believe in Spiritualism are daily increasing, and the purblind policy of ignoring its principles and action must very soon come to an end. Of course Materialists and sceptics reasonably doubt; for otherwise their own infallibility would ignominiously collapse. But for Christians, who possess a copy of the " Holy Bible," and are able to read it, doubt seems to me (I write with all due humility) simply inconsequent and irrational.

Here, let us turn from shadow to sunshine, from that which is evil to that which is good; from the "lying wonders" of designing evil spirits, to the glorious manifestations of God Almighty's power in the Christian Church—for the one kind are but reasonable correlatives of the other.

And, for myself, I am free to confess that the evidence in favour of certain of the recent miracles said to have been wrought in the Roman Catholic portion of the One Family of God is not only convincing, but conclusive. Having long given up attributing any value to the slanders and misstatements of Protestant and infidel writers, I have attempted for myself to investigate the principle of action, in the reception of evidence and the decision of authority, which is taken at Rome, with regard to such events and occurrences; and briefly give it as follows :—

The Congregation of Rites, which enquires into all miracles which demand sanction, is presided over by the cardinal-vicar. It consists of twenty-one cardinals of various nations, nine official prelates, nine consulting prelates of various nations, all the fourteen Papal Masters of Ceremonies, fourteen ordinary members, one secretary, one deputy-secretary, and one notary and keeper of the archives —in all seventy people. Four miracles are required to be distinctly proved for Beatification; and two more for Canonization. All these must be proved by eye, and not by ear-witnesses. In miracles where diseases have been cured, it is required, 1st, That the disease must have been of an aggravated nature, and difficult or impossible to be cured; 2ndly, that it was not on the turn; 3rdly, that no medicine had been used, or if it had that it had done no good; 4thly, the cure must be sudden; 5thly, it must be complete and perfect; and 6thly, there must have been no crisis. In the process of examination and enquiry, no step is taken, no doubt propounded, no fact allowed, without many of the members of the Congregation being present: and a printed Report is sent to all who may have been absent. Besides the ordinary cross-examinations, which are always of a most scrutinizing character, it is the sole duty of one of the leading members of the Congregation, the *Promotor Fidei*, as he is termed, to raise objections, and if possible to disprove every reported miracle. The members of this Congregation are as keen, penetrating and business-like, and have as complete a knowledge of the unconscious delusions of the human heart, as any body of English jurymen. As ecclesiastical scholars they may be truly said to be equal to the same number of English barristers; and the head of the Congregation, for shrewdness, acuteness of intellect, and judicial ability, is equal to any judge in England, who by his interpretation of the law, and his particular sentence in a special case, wills away the life or property of any Englishman. The subject has been treated at length in the great work of Pope Benedict XIV. (A.D. 1740-1758) "On Beatification," &c., as well as in the Decrees of Pope Urban VIII. and Pope Clement XI.; and so sifting and careful has always been the investigation, that Alban Butler asserts, on the authority of Daubenton, that an English gentleman (not a Roman Catholic) being present and seeing the process of several miracles, maintained them to have been completely proved and perfectly incontestable, but was astonished beyond measure at the scrupulosity of the scrutiny when authoritatively informed that *not one of those which he had heard discussed* had been allowed by the Congregation to have been sufficiently proved.

Father Perrone, the distinguished living theologian, also asserts that having shown the formal process for certain miracles to a lawyer of some eminence (not a Roman Catholic) who after examination was perfectly satisfied with both the testimony and the reasoning, the latter declared that they would certainly stand before a British jury; but was mightily astonished on hearing that the Congregation did not consider that evidence to be sufficiently convincing and conclusive.

Similar investigations have been made in England, since the Reformation, and this by ecclesiastical authority. For example: in the year before his translation to the see of Norwich (*i.e.* in 1640), Dr. Joseph Hall, then Bishop of Exeter, made a strict and judicial inquiry into all the circumstances of the sudden and miraculous cure of a cripple at S. Madron's Well, in Cornwall, and the following is the recorded conviction of this pious prelate:—
" The commerce which we have with the good spirits is not now discerned by the eye, but is, like themselves, spiritual. Yet not so, but that even in bodily occasions we have many times insensible helps from them; in such a manner as that by the effects we can boldly say, ' Here hath been an angel, though we see him not.' Of this kind was that (no less than miraculous) cure which at S. Madron's, in Cornwall, was wrought upon a poor cripple, John Trelille, where (besides the attestation of many hundreds of neighbours), I took a strict and personal examination in that last Visitation which I ever did or ever shall hold. This man, that for sixteen years together was fain to walk upon his hands, by reason of the close contraction of the sinews of his legs, (upon three admonitions in a dream to wash in that well) was suddenly so restored to his limbs, that I

THE SUPERNATURAL. 231

saw him able to walk and get his own maintenance. I found here was neither art nor collusion: the thing done, the author invisible."[1]

Now, whatever may be thought of the principles enunciated in Mr. Lecky's[2] volumes on "The Rise and Influence of Rationalism," none can deny either the marvellous faculty exhibited for gathering and marshalling facts; while some portions of his thoughtful reflections do but put into luminous language thoughts and convictions which find a cordial response from many.

The following remarkable passage is singularly true and accurate in its estimate of an unmistakeable historical fact, viz., that the Oxford movement to a great extent left out of consideration[3] the continued

---

[1] "On the Invisible World," by Joseph Hall, D.D., &c., book i. sec. 8. Father Christopher Davenport, better known as "Sancta Clara," in one of his most remarkable treatises, "Paralipomena Philosophica de Mundo Peripatetico," chap. iv. p. 68 (A.D. 1652), confirms the account in the text of the above-named Bishop of Exeter, giving all the details of this particular miraculous cure. It seems that both the Well and Chapel of S. Madron were constantly visited by the faithful during the first part of the seventeenth century, especially in the month of May and on the feast of Corpus Christi.

[2] "History of the Rise and Influence of the Spirit of Rationalism in Europe," by W. E. H. Lecky, M.A. Fourth edition in two volumes. London, 1870.

[3] Dr. Newman will, of course, be excepted; for his remarkable Dissertation prefixed to the translation of Fleury's "History" is known to many, more especially in its new form,—a volume already referred to at length in chap. ii. pp. 35-36. It is certainly quite unjust to include the Tractarian

existence of modern miracles in the Christian Church. Mr. Lecky writes thus:—"At Oxford these narratives (*i.e.* the record of patristic and mediæval miracles) hardly exercised a serious attention. What little influence they had was chiefly an influence of repression; what little was written in their favour was written for the most part in the tone of an apology, as if to attenuate a difficulty rather than to establish a creed. This was surely a very remarkable characteristic of the Tractarian movement, when we remember the circumstances and attainments of its leaders, and the great prominence which miraculous evidence had long occupied in England. It was especially remarkable when we reflect that one of the great complaints which the Tractarian party were making against modern theology was, that the conception of the Supernatural had become faint and dim, and that its manifestations were either explained away or confined to a distant past. It would seem as if those who were most conscious of the character of their age were unable, in the very midst of their

---

school amongst those who are referred to by Mr. Lecky in the following passage:—" At present nearly all educated men receive an account of a miracle taking place in their own day, with an absolute and even derisive incredulity which dispenses with all examination of the evidence."—Vol. i. p. 1. Though many are reticent, and many more shrink from publicity and rude criticism, it is known that the direct influence of the Miraculous and Supernatural is by no means unknown in the Church of England.

opposition, to free themselves from its tendencies."
—Vol. i. pp. 165-166.

It must be allowed that there is some amount of truth in this temperately-made charge. Whatever else may have been pressed forward, and with success, it is obvious that the active energy of the Supernatural has been kept somewhat in the background. At all events it has not been made too prominent. Even in books of devotion, adapted from Roman Catholic sources, examples of miracles have been omitted; and so the golden threads which were so rudely broken three centuries and a half ago, are still in the mire; for few have cared to gather them up once more and weave them into a perfect whole. That work has still to be done. Not until there be what a modern writer terms "daring faith"—faith which can move mountains—should the work be attempted.

And now, fully alive to its imperfections, I bring my book to its close.

It has been briefly shown herein what a great influence the materialistic speculations of a few bold and over-confident writers have recently exercised on current thought. At the same time the presence of the Supernatural in Church History has been made perfectly manifest, and abundant sources pointed out from which additional examples may readily be gathered for consideration by those who may desire to gather them. Side by side, however, with that which in the Supernatural order is good and beneficial to man, energizes that which is evil. There are angels and there are demons. There is light and there is darkness. Numberless armies of glorious spirits, as the Divine Revelation tells us,[1] stand, rank by rank and order by order, as the bright ornaments of the City of God. Their subtlety, their quickness of penetration, their extensive knowledge of natural things, are undoubtedly perfect in proportion to the excellency of their being, inasmuch as they are pure intelligences, perfect from the Hand of their Maker. They know the concerns of mortal men.[2] They are our protectors, our patrons, our guides. For us they lift up their prayers to God, and they are near us in our trials and temptations. Their motion is swift as thought, their activity inconceivable. As they are the friends of mankind by God's decree, so specially do they become the guardians of the regenerate and the particular protectors of the innocent and young. And their beneficent actions are not altogether unknown. The old records tell of their charity; man's experience testifies to their presence. And, furthermore, for man's behoof in his time of trial, and for his eternal advantage hereafter, were given those

---

[1] Job xxv. 5.
[2] See a most remarkable Letter from the pen of my friend the Rev. R. S. Hawker, of Morwenstow, on "The Claims of Science and Faith," standing as an Appendix to this Chapter, in which the office of the angels is referred to.

powers and properties which belong to the Church by the grace and efficacy of the Sacraments.

Yet, on the other hand, until the number of the Elect is accomplished, the Enemy of Souls, the Prince of the Powers of the Air, is permitted to wield an alarming influence; while too often the natural man, with his will free, wills to remain his servant. Yea; and even the baptized, too. For by Witchcraft, Sorcery, and Necromancy Satan still works, men being his direct agents and slaves. Sometimes in one form, sometimes in another, he dupes those who seek him; while his legions suggest to men's minds evil thoughts, paint dangerous objects to the imagination, frequently direct the active current of the human heart to sin, and finally turn round and accuse their captives at the tribunal of God the Judge of all. So must it be to the end, for this life is man's time of probation.

Of Dreams and Warnings, Omens and Presentiments, much has been written. Each example must be considered on its own merits; for perhaps no coherent theory will sufficiently cover and explain all the instances here already adduced.

So, too, with Spectral Appearances and Haunted Localities. While experience testifies to the facts recorded, such Glimpses of the Supernatural may be well left to tell their own story, to leave their own impression, and set forth their own teaching. To those who possess the grace and habit of faith they will not seem over-strange, for as Hamlet remarked to his friend—

> " There are more things in Heaven and Earth, Horatio,
> Than are dreamt of in our philosophy."

As I prepare to lay down my pen, I cannot but notice and put on record what amid "the triumphs of Science," so frequently start up to confront us, viz. the sad records of calamity brought to notice, and the gloomy scenes of deepest misery which are yet so frequently depicted. "Woe is me!" is man's wail still. But with many the Supernatural, as we too well know, is bidden to stand aside. The Catholic Religion is written of as antiquated, out of date, and effete. The truth of the Christian Revelation is openly denied. Yet may not the terrible disasters of which we hear, and the miserable calamities which so constantly occur along the path of "human progress" and "scientific triumph," be permitted by God Almighty as an intelligible and richly deserved rebuke to lofty looks and the impious and blasphemous thoughts of the proud?[1]

---

[1] Mr. Mill, who is now dead, wrote that "this World was a bungled business in which no clear-sighted man [meaning himself apparently, and modestly] could see any signs either of wisdom or of God." Mr. Matthew Arnold, son of Dr. Arnold of Rugby, has written that "the existence of God is an unverifiable hypothesis." A third writer maintains that the "great duty" of the philosophers "should be to eliminate

Man's life in this country is certainly not longer than it was eight or ten centuries ago. He dies as he died. Nor is the race of Englishmen sturdier, finer, or better grown than of old. The tombs of the Crusaders tell us this. Look at the stately figures of the Fitzalans in Bedale Church, or at those of the Marmions in that of Tanfield, and it may be that in this practical particular deterioration instead of progress should be more fittingly and faithfully recorded. As is obvious enough, Science, with all the boasting of its adherents, can, after all, effect but little. True it is that wonderful discoveries are made in the Realms of Nature. Operations untraced before, are now accurately apprehended; and secrets, long hidden, are triumphantly brought to light. One might imagine from the random confidence of some (as guides more shallow than safe), that Science had discovered an appliance for every human weakness, an antidote to every physical evil or disease, an unfailing specific against every want and woe. Yet, after all its researches and with all its supposed discoveries (for many may have been known

---

the idea of God from the minds of men," a sentiment not unlike that of Mr. Congreve, already quoted on p. 19 of vol. i.; while a popular publication, circulated by thousands amongst the lower classes, declares that the mission of its Editors is "to teach men to live without the fear of God; to die without the fear of the Devil; and to attain salvation without the Blood of the Lamb."

and lost), never were failures so great or misfortunes so heavy. The ugly iron ship of the present day, hideous in form and appearance, yet constructed with all the obtainable skill of modern science, at an enormous sacrifice of expense, fitted with life-boats and patent scientific life-preservers, divided into compartments, after due calculations (on a scientific method), suddenly goes down, where a fisherman of six centuries ago, in his wooden skiff, would have ridden a storm securely, and becomes an iron coffin for five or six hundred corpses, rotting where the seaweed grows. Again, War, with scientific appliances—in the invention and preparation of which the great nations are active rivals—marches over a great country, defended by the highest military art and strength, and in a few short months reduces its people to spoliation, tribute, and shame. Less than a century ago, nearly a twenty years' struggle would have been made, ere such a sudden and sweeping contest could have been so securely sealed.

Human Art may do something, and Science may effect more: but how frequently some little flaw or casualty defeats all! The boastings of Science, consequently, become vain and vapid: its works lie in the dust. Past ages have had their pride humbled; as Tyre and Alexandria and Babylon too eloquently tell. When God, by the insolence of intellect, is thrust aside, He sometimes, nevertheless, mercifully but efficiently reminds men that

He is. When the Supernatural is deliberately denied and scornfully rejected, suffering may serve to open the eyes of the blind and make the dumb to speak. The general tendency in these days is to worship Mind, Intelligence, and Power, for Might, with too many, is Right. Literary jargon setting forth this duty may be constantly read. The wisest action for the truly wise is to turn away from such; for the noblest and proudest ambition of a Christian's life should consist in being humble worshippers of Him the One Author of the Supernatural and the Natural, Whose only power is infinite, Whose knowledge and wisdom are boundless, and Whose abiding love and mercy are over all His works.

Appendix to Chapter X.

THE CLAIMS OF SCIENCE AND FAITH.

BY my friend Mr. Hawker's obliging kindness I am enabled to publish the following remarkable Letter:—

"To Mr. S. J——, Merchant, Plymouth.

"My Dear Nephew,—You ask me 'to put into one of my nutshells' the pith and marrow of the controversy which at this time pervades the English mind as to the claims of Science and Faith. Let me try: The material universe—so the sages allege—is a vast assemblage of atoms or molecules—'motes in the sunbeam' of Science, which has existed for myriads of ages under a perpetual system of evolution, restructure, and change. This mighty mass is traversed by the forces electrical, or magnetic, or with other kindred names; and these by their incessant and indomitable action are adequate to account for all the phenomena of the world of matter, and of man. The upheaval of a continent; the drainage of a sea; the creation of a metal; nay, the origin of life, and the development of a species in plant, or animal, or man; these are the achievements of fixed and natural laws among the atomic materials, under the vibration of the forces alone. Thus far the vaunted discoveries of Science are said to have arrived. Let us indulge them with the theory that these results, for they are nothing more, are accurate and real. But still, a thoughtful mind will venture to demand whence did these atoms derive their existence? and from what, and from whom, do they inherit the propensities wherewithal they are imbued? And tell me, most potent seigniors, what is the origin of these forces? And with whom resides the impulse of their action and the guidance of their control? 'Nothing so difficult as a beginning.' Your philosopher is mute! he has reached the horizon of his domain, and to him all beyond is doubt, and uncertainty, and guess. We must lift the veil. We must pass into the border-land between two Worlds, and there inquire at the Oracles of Revelation touching the Unseen and Spiritual powers which thrill through the mighty sacrament of the visible Creation. We perceive, being inspired, the realms of surrounding space peopled by immortal creatures of air—

> 'Myriads of spiritual things that walk unseen,
> Both when we wake and when we sleep.'

These are the existences, in aspect as 'young men in white garments,' who inhabit the void place between the

Worlds and their Maker, and their God. Behold the battalions of the Lord of Hosts! the Workers of the sky! the faithful and intelligent Vassals of God the Trinity! We have named them in our own poor and meagre language 'the Angels,' but this title merely denotes one of their subordinate offices—messengers from on high. The Gentiles called them 'Gods,' but we ought to honour them by a name that should embrace and interpret their lofty dignity as an intermediate army between the kingdom and the throne; the Centurions of the stars, and of men; the Commanders of the forces and their Guides. These are they that, each with a delegated office, fulfil what their 'King invisible' decrees; not with the dull, inert mechanism of fixed and natural law, but with the unslumbering energy and the rational obedience of spiritual life. They mould the atom; they wield the force; and, as Newton rightly guessed, they rule the World of matter beneath the silent Omnipotence of God.

"'And he dreamed, and behold a ladder set up on the earth, and the top of it reached to Heaven; and behold the angels of God ascending and descending on it. And behold the Lord stood above it.'—Genesis xxviii. 12. *Tolle, Lege,* my dear nephew.

"Your affectionate uncle,

"R. S. HAWKER.

"Morwenstow Vicarage, Cornwall."

GENERAL INDEX.

 DISCERNER of spirits, i. 81
Abimelech's dream, i. 210
Aerolites, i. 24
After-vision of a suicide, ii. 75
Alexander Macdonald's dream, i. 285
Amulet of the Grahams, i. 277
—— of the Macdonald Lockharts, i. 278
Ann Thorne bewitched, i. 194
Apparition at Ballarat, ii. 61
—— at time of death, ii. 59
—— in the Jewel House, ii. 105
—— near Cardiff, ii. 114
—— of a college friend, ii. 71
—— of a crow, ii. 131
—— of a dying father, ii. 58
—— of a dying lady to her children, ii. 64
—— of a father to his son, ii. 58
—— of a friend, ii. 60
—— of a sister, ii. 59
—— of a son to his mother and another, ii. 73
—— of an officer, ii. 10
—— of Dr. Ferrar's daughter, ii. 25
—— of Philip Weld, ii. 51
—— of Rev. W. Naylor, ii. 7
—— of S. Stanislaus, ii. 51
—— seven years after death, ii. 71
—— to a gentleman, ii. 119

Apparition to a lady and her child, ii. 113
—— to a lady and her child, ii. 117
—— to a sentry, and his death thereupon, ii. 108
—— to Lord Brougham, ii. 68
—— to Lord Chedworth, ii. 35
—— to Mr. Andrews, ii. 41
Apparitions at Oxford, ii. 209
Arrowsmith, Trial of Rev. E., i. 91
Arrowsmith's Hand preserved, i. 95
Authentication of Lamb's cure, i. 96
Barony of Chedworth, ii. 34
Belief in God universal, i. 5
Benediction, The principle of, i. 90
Beresford apparition, The, ii. 11
Bird, The Spectral, ii. 128
Bisham Abbey, Ghost at, ii. 91
Bishop Joseph Hall on temporal punishment, ii. 89
Bishop Ken's hymn, ii. 82
Blessing and cursing, Power of, i. 90
Bosworth's testimony, Mr. T., ii. 146
Bridget Bishop accused of witchcraft, i. 198
Bull of Pope Innocent VIII. against witchcraft, i. 162
Captain William Dyke, ii. 22

Cardan, Jerome, i. 282
Case of Annie Milner, i. 169
—— of Martha Brossier, i. 165
Catharine Campbell accused of witchcraft, i. 197
Catholic claim to exclusive use of exorcism, i. 163
Causation, The law of, i. 3
Chamber, John, on "Judiciall Astrologie," i. 200
Charles I., Omens concerning, i. 267, 271
Charles Ireland bewitched, i. 186
Chevalier's testimony concerning Spiritualism, Mr., ii. 180
"Christ is coming" quoted, ii. 136
Christian Shaw bewitched, i. 197
Christian writers on the Supernatural, i. 31
Christianity, Morse on the decline of, ii. 137
Citation, Remarkable case of, i. 90
Club, The Hell-Fire, ii. 207
Colgarth, The Philipsons of, i. 90
Collins's Sermon, Rev. H., i. 135
Cometism, The Trinity of, i. 19
Constantine victorious, i. 38
Creslow, Haunted chamber at, ii. 92
Criticism upon Mr. Congreve, i. 20
Crookes, Mr. W., on Spiritualism, ii. 159, 162, 164
Cross of Constantine, The, i. 35
—— fire seen in France in 1826, A, i. 16
Cure, Miraculous, i. 95
—— Miraculous, by the Blessed Sacrament, i. 121, 125
Daimonomagia, i. 174
Dale-Owen, Mr., quoted, ii. 183, 185
Death of Captain Speer, i. 253
—— of Rev. S. B. Drury, i. 251
De Lisle's, Miss, death, Supernatural music at, i. 135
De Lisle, Mr., on the Weld ghost story, ii. 54
—— Mr. Edwin, on Strauss, i. 2

Demons, Belief in, ii. 212
Denial of the Supernatural, i. 1
Details of the Supernatural, i. 8
Discovery of a lost will, i. 204
Disease of witchcraft, i. 174
Double apparition at time of death, ii. 55
—— in the West Indies, ii. 58
Dr. Lamb, the sorcerer, i. 202
Dr. Newman on ecclesiastical miracles, i. 36
Dr. Samuel Johnson on the Lyttelton story, ii. 45
Dr. William Harvey's escape from death, i. 284
Dream of a child, Warning given in the, i. 260
—— of a dignitary realized, i. 257
—— of a housekeeper realized, i. 240
—— of a widow lady, i. 258
—— of Adam Rogers, i. 219
—— of Andrew Scott, i. 261
—— of Mr. Matthew Talbot, i. 225
—— of Mr. Williams of Scorrier, i. 226
—— of the Princess Natgotsky, i. 255
—— of the Swaffham tinker, i. 215
—— Prognostication of death in a, i. 250
—— Remarkable, of a clergyman, i. 247
—— Warning given in a, i. 254
—— Warning neglected, i. 244
Dreams and visions, i. 211
Dreams, Nature of, i. 210
—— of James Jessop, i. 244, 245
—— recorded in Scripture, i. 211
—— reproduction of thoughts in, i. 215
—— supernatural, i. 210
Dunbar's testimony, Rev. Dr., ii. 218
Dungeon at Glamis Castle, The, ii. 114
Early Popes martyrs, The, i. 31
Eastern form of exorcism, i. 162
Ecclesiastical miracles, i. 32
Effect of the Supernatural, i. 7

GENERAL INDEX.

Elimination of God, The, i. 19
Elizabeth Gorham bewitched, i. 187
—— Style accused of witchcraft, i. 177
—— Tibbots bewitched, i. 178
—— Treslar hung for witchcraft, i. 181
Ellinor Shaw and Mary Philips, i. 182
Emperor Julian thwarted, The, i. 42
English canon concerning exorcism, i. 164
—— statutes against witchcraft, i. 163
"Eternal," The term, i. 5
Execution of Frederick Caulfield, i. 223
—— of Lamb's servant, i. 203
Exhumation of James Quin, i. 236
Exorcism, Power of, i. 57, 69, 82
—— Latin form of, i. 138
—— Oriental form of, i. 162
Facts of witchcraft and necromancy, i. 164
Faculty of Jerome Cardan, i. 283
Fall of aerolites, i. 25
False reasoning, i. 26
Ferrers family, Omen concerning, i. 272
Florence Newton accused of witchcraft, i. 180
Friday an unlucky day, i. 282
Ghost of Bisham Abbey, ii. 91
God and His creatures, i. 4
—— The elimination of, i. 19
Guesses of Science, The, i. 14
Hand of Arrowsmith preserved, i. 95
Hanmer, Mr. C. L., on an apparition, ii. 60
Hannah Green's testimony, i. 242
Haunted houses and localities, ii. 82
—— chamber at Creslow, ii. 92
—— Glamis Castle, ii. 114
—— house at Barby, ii. 109
—— house at Berne, ii. 126
—— house in Cheshire, ii. 116
—— house in Scotland, ii. 123

Haunted place at York Castle, ii. 96
—— places, ii. 84
—— police cell, ii. 121
—— road near Cardiff, ii. 114
—— room at Glamis Castle, ii. 112
—— room in the Tower, ii. 104
—— spot in Yorkshire, ii. 100
Hell-Fire Club, The, ii. 207
Henry Spicer's testimony, Mr., ii. 75
—— IV. of France, Omen of death to, i. 267
Herder on Witchcraft, ii. 210
Heresies of the modern Spiritualists, ii. 185, 191
Home, Mr. Daniel, ii. 151, 153
Hospitals, Christian in their origin, i. 10
Howell, Mr. J., on Spiritualism, ii. 176, 177
Howitt, Mr. W., on eternal punishment, ii. 186, 188
Hume on miracles, i. 23
Increase Mather on the tests of demoniacal possession, i. 173
—— Mather's "Cases of Conscience," i. 195
Inquiries regarding Wynyard, ii. 33
Jane Brookes accused of witchcraft, i. 175
—— Wenham accused of witchcraft, i. 192
Johnson, Dr. Samuel, on the Lyttelton ghost, ii. 45.
Kostka's, S. Stanislaus, apparition, ii. 53
—— picture at Stonyhurst, ii. 53
Labarum, The, i. 37
Lactantius on dreams, i. 213
Lady Betty Cobb, ii. 15
Lancashire demoniacs, The, i. 171
Lane, Mr., on Modern Necromancy, ii. 215, 217
Laud, Omens concerning Archbishop, i. 271
Law of causation, The, i. 3
Lecky, Mr. W. H. E., on the Oxford Movement, ii. 232
Legion, The Thundering, i. 34

Longdon, Mary, bewitched, i. 194
Lord Falkland, Omen concerning, i. 270
Lord Litchfield's note of a presentiment, i. 281
—— testimony, i. 281
Lord Westcote's testimony, ii. 42
Lyttelton Ghost story, ii. 36, 42, 46
Macdonald's, A., case of second sight, i. 285
Macknish on dreams, i. 215
Major George Sydenham, ii. 22
Marquis de Marsay on Spirits, ii. 86
Mary of Medicis, Omen of death to, i. 267
Media, Table of Spiritual, ii. 143
Mines, Haunted, ii. 84
Ministry of Angels, ii. 82
Miracles at Rome in 1792, i. 17
—— Bishop Hall on, ii. 230
—— examination of at Rome, ii. 227
—— of our Lord, i. 30
—— of Prince Hohenlohe, i. 17
—— wrought by the Blessed Sacrament, i. 123, 126
Miracle at Garswood, i. 96
—— at Metz, i. 128
—— at Typasa, i. 42
—— under Marcus Aurelius, i. 33
Miraculous cure at Pontoise, i. 83
—— facts, Tradition of, i. 32
—— of Joseph Lamb, i. 95
—— of Mary Wood, i. 114
—— of Winifred White, i. 116
Mediumship, ii. 143
—— Clairlative, ii. 146
—— Clairvoyant, ii. 150
—— Developing, ii. 148
—— Duodynamic, ii. 148
—— Gesticulating, ii. 144
—— Homo-motor, ii. 147
—— Impersonating, ii. 145
—— Impressional, ii. 150
—— Manipulating, ii. 145
—— Missionary, ii. 149
—— Motive, ii. 144
—— Neurological, ii. 146
—— Pantomimic, ii. 145
—— Pictorial, ii. 148

Mediumship, Psychologic, ii. 147
—— Psychometric, ii. 148
—— Pulsatory, ii. 145.
—— Speaking, ii. 150
—— Symbolic, ii. 147
—— Sympathetic, ii. 146
—— Therapeutic, ii. 149
—— Tipping, ii. 144
—— Vibratory, ii. 144
Miss Weld's testimony, ii. 54
Modern scientific methods, i. 10
Monsignor Patterson's testimony, ii. 52
More's "Antidote against Atheism," i. 173
Mr. De Lisle on Miracles, i. 15
Mr. De Lisle's testimony, ii. 54
Mr. Edwin De Lisle in reply to Strauss, i. 4
Mr. E. Lenthal Swifte's testimony, ii. 104
Mr. George Fortescue's declaration, ii. 43
Mr. Henry Cope Caulfeild's testimony, ii. 115
Mr. Herbert Spencer answered, i. 11
Mr. J. G. Godwin's declaration, ii. 68
Mr. Laxon's wife tormented, i. 189
Mr. M. P. Andrews' declaration, ii. 43
Mr. Ralph Davis on the Northampton witches, i. 182
Mr. Rutherford's declaration, i. 263
Mr. William Talbot's testimony, i. 226
Mrs. Baillie-Hamilton's testimony, ii. 66
Mrs. George Lee's testimony, i. 230
Mrs. Kempson's testimony, i. 254
Murder discovered by a dream, i. 221
—— of Maria Martin discovered, i. 231
—— of the crippled and imbecile, i. 9
Naturalistic materialism, i. 10
Nature of God, i. 6

Nature of dreams, i. 210
Necromancy recognized by the fathers, i. 161
—— in China, ii. 220
Northamptonshire witches, The, i. 182
Notions, reintroduction of Pagan, i. 13
Old traditions generally accepted, ii. 90
Omen concerning Archbishop Laud, i. 271
—— concerning King Charles I., i. 268, 269, 270
—— concerning Lord Falkland, i. 270
Omens and prognostications, i. 263
—— The subject of, i. 263
Opinions of Strauss, i. 3
Oracles, The cessation of, i. 282
Ostrehan's, Captain, testimony, ii. 218
Oxenham omen, The, i. 273
Pagan notions, Reintroduction of, i. 13
Patterson's, Monsignor, information, ii. 52
Perrone, Father, on Spiritualism, ii. 184
Philipsons of Colgarth, The, i. 90
Planchette, Use of, ii. 220, 222
Plumer Ward's, Mr., account of the Lyttelton ghost, ii. 46
Plutarch on the "Cessation of Oracles," i. 282
Popes martyrs, The early, i. 31
Portrait of S. Stanislaus, ii. 53
Power and malice of Satan, ii. 83
—— of blessing and cursing, i. 90
—— of exorcism claimed exclusively, i. 163
Presentiment of Lieutenant R—, i. 250
—— of death, i. 262
—— to Lady Warre's chaplain, i. 281
Principle of benediction, The, i. 88
Principles of the Broad Church party, ii. 137

Prognostication of death in a dream, i. 250
—— of death to Captain Speer, i. 252
Prognostications and omens, i. 263
Propriety of a revelation, i. 5
Purbrick, Rev. E. J., on the Weld ghost story, ii. 54
Purport of dreams, i. 212
Rebuilding of the Temple, i. 42
"Report on Spiritualism" quoted, ii. 153
Rev. Dr. Cox's testimony, ii. 54
Rev. Dr. J. M. Neale's testimony, i. 243
Rev. Edward Price on the World of Spirits, ii. 82
Rev. G. R. Winter on the Swaffham tinker, i. 215
Rev. H. N. Oxenham's testimony, i. 277
Rev. J. Richardson's testimony, i. 253
Rev. John Wesley on evil spirits, ii. 85
Rev. Joseph Jefferson's testimony, ii. 100
Rev. Mr. Perring's dream realized, i. 234
Rev. T. J. Morris's testimony, i. 240
"Rules for the Spirit Circle" quoted, ii. 151
S. Augustine on miracles, i. 30
S. Bernard on dreams, i. 214
S. Cyprian on dreams, i. 214
S. Cyril on dreams, i. 214
S. Irenæus on miracles, i. 41
S. John's College, Oxford, Founding of, i. 267
S. Pacian on miracles, i. 41
S. Thomas Aquinas on dreams, i. 214
Sacrilege discovered by a dream, i. 232
"Sadducismus Triumphatus" referred to, i. 199
Satan, power and malice of, ii. 83
Science and faith, Rev. R. S. Hawker on, ii. 239

Science of the Pagan oracles, i. 161
"Scientific View of Modern Spiritualism" quoted, ii. 143
Scott, Dream of Andrew, i. 261
Scripture on witchcraft and necromancy, i. 164
Séance at the Marshalls', i. 203
—— record of, from "Spiritual Magazine," ii. 169
Second sight, Treatise on, i. 285
—— at Cardiff, i. 286
—— at Ramsbury, i. 288
—— Jerome Cardan's gift of, i. 283
Sexton, Dr. G., on spiritualism, ii. 225
Shakespeare's conception of the supernatural, ii. 89
Singular prognostication, i. 250
Sir Christopher Heydon on astrology, i. 200
Sir George Caulfeild, i. 223
Sir Henry Chauncy trying witches, i. 193
Sir Henry Yelverton and his death, i. 95
Sir Martin Beresford, ii. 13
Sir Matthew Hale's evidence as to witchcraft, i. 163
Sir Thomas Brown's evidence against witchcraft, i. 163
Slade's, Sir Alfred, testimony, ii. 218
Somerset omen, The, i. 266
Sorcery of Dr. Lamb, i. 202
Sortes Virgilianæ, The, i. 269, 270
Sound of a drum, The, i. 278
Southey on haunted localities, ii. 84
Spectral dog, The, i. 280
Spectre of Lady Hobby, The, ii. 91
Spedlin's Tower haunted, ii. 97
Spirits, perturbed, ii. 87
—— World of, ii. 82
Spiritualism despised, ii. 139
—— modern, ii. 135, 169
—— Mr. W. Crookes on the phenomena of, ii. 159

Spiritualism, Origin of, ii. 141
Spiritualistic manifestations, i. 205; ii. 151, 153, 155, 157, 160, 161, 163, 169, 173, 175, 176, 177, 178, 180
Statement of Lord Lyttelton's valet, ii. 45
Stigmatization, i. 98, 100, 101, 102, 105, 109
Strauss, Opinions of,' i. 2
Successful exorcism by an English clergyman, i. 80
Sudden death of Ruth Pierce, i. 289
Supernatural banished, The, ii. 140
—— basis of life, i. 12
—— its work, i. 2
—— noises at Abbotsford, ii. 99
—— religion, i. 18
Surey demoniac, The, i. 177
Tertullian on dreams, i. 213
Testimony to the fulfilment of a solemn Curse, i. 117
The Chester-le-Street apparition, ii. 3
The Christian system, i. 26
The Lyttelton ghost story, ii. 35
The Misses Amphlett, ii. 39
The Oxenham omen, i. 274
The result of a solemn Curse, i. 117
The sound of a drum, i. 278
The spectral dog, i. 280
—— bird, ii. 128
The use of the Sign of the Cross, ii. 4
The white bird of the Oxenhams, i. 274
Theories concerning dreams, i. 210
Thirteen to Dinner, i. 281
Thomas Aquinas on miracles, S., i. 28
Three men rescued by a dream, i. 231
Tichborne dole, The, i. 264
—— Curse and Prophecy, The, i. 265
—— Mabella, Lady, i. 264
—— Sir Henry, i. 265
—— Sir Roger, i. 264

Tinley, Dream of Samuel, i. 262
Tradition of miraculous powers, i. 32
Treatise on second sight, i. 285
Trial of Rev. E. Arrowsmith, i. 91
Trinity of Comteism, The, i. 19
Twice-repeated dream of a sailor, i. 231
Tyrone apparition, The, ii. 11
Unalterable experience, i. 24
Use of the Sign of the Cross, ii. 4
Wallace, Mr. A., on spiritualism and science, ii. 193
Wandering souls, ii. 87
Ward's account of the Lyttelton ghost, Mr., ii. 46
Warning given in a dream, i. 238, 254
—— given to a lady by a dream, i. 242
—— to a lady, i. 258
—— to a little child, i. 260
—— to two persons in dreams, i. 258
"Weekly Register," The, on Mr. Wallace's theories, ii. 197
Weld ghost story, The, ii. 49
—— Philip, drowned, ii. 50
—— Very Rev. Alfred, S. J., on the Weld ghost story, ii. 54

Weld's, Philip, apparition, ii. 53
Westcote, Lord, on the Lyttelton ghost, i. 33
White's Dream, Sir Thomas, i. 266
Witchcraft and necromancy, i. 152
—— and sorcery, Canon Melville on, i. 156
—— common in non-Catholic countries, i. 201
—— condemned in Scripture, i. 152, 155
—— Definition of, i. 174
—— Examples of, i. 176—201
—— George More on, i. 171
—— Herder on, ii. 210
—— Jane Wenham accused of, i. 192
—— Joseph Glanville on, i. 175
—— recognized by the Fathers, i. 161
—— Rev. John Wesley on, i. 160
Witches, The Northamptonshire, i. 182
"Wonders of the Invisible World," i. 198
World of spirits, The, ii. 82
Wynyard ghost story, The, ii. 26

THE END.

www.ingramcontent.com/pod-product-compliance
Lightning Source LLC
Chambersburg PA
CBHW020755230426
43666CB00007B/709